Veggie Burgers:

150 Delicious Vegan Burger Recipes

Julian Holden

Please Note:

Copyright © 2016 by Project Inspiration. All rights reserved worldwide. No part of this publication may be reproduced or transmitted in any form without the prior written consent of the publisher.

Limit of Liability/Disclaimer of Warranty: The publisher and author make no representations or warranties with respect to the accuracy or completeness of these contents and disclaim all warranties such as warranties of fitness for a particular purpose. The author or publisher is not liable for any damages whatsoever. The fact that an individual or organization is referred to in this document as a citation or source of information does not imply that the author or publisher endorses the information that the individual or organization provided. This concise recipe guide is unofficial and is not authorized, approved, licensed, or endorsed by any other author promoting Vegan Recipes.

Table of Contents

Veggie Burgers i

Vegan burger buns!! 1
Lentil Oatmeal Burgers 2
White/Black Bean Burgers 3
Lentil/Pea Burgers with Cayenne 4
Eggplant Pesto Burgers 5
Cauliflower Burgers with Curry 7
Black Bean Mushroom Burgers 8
Powerful Green Burgers 9
Portobello Burgers with Balsamic Vinegar 10
Cayenne Chickpea Burgers 11
Potato Burgers 12
Bean Mushroom Burgers 13
Kidney Bean Burgers with Pumpkin Seeds 14
Eggplant Tomato Burgers 15
Mushroom Burgers 16
Black Bean/Broccoli Burgers 17
Zucchini Balsamic Vinegar Burgers 18
Sweet Potato and Bean Burgers 19
Tofu Portobello Burgers 20
Mushroom Pineapple Burgers 21
Chickpeas Burgers 22
Quinoa Pepper Burgers 23

Portobello Onion Burgers 24
Tropical Island Burgers..25
Tofu Almond Burgers..26
Mushroom Broccoli Burgers..27
Sweet Corn/Potato Burgers..28
Spicy Thai Burger 29
Summer Squash Burgers..31
Pineapple Buckwheat Burgers 32
Broccoli Leak Burgers 33
Soybean Burgers..34
Tofu Marmalade Burgers...35
Spinach and Pistachio Burgers 36

Fried Burgers
Pinto Burgers with Chipotle Aioli..39
Fennel and Beetroot Burger 41
Mushroom Chickpea Burgers..42
Sweet Corn Burgers with Chickpea 43
Fried Potato and Garlic Burgers..44
Spicy Nut and Seed Burgers 45
Quinoa Beet Burgers 46
Spicy Black Bean Burgers 47
Carrot Quinoa Burgers..48
Spicy Chickpea Oat Burgers..49
Cashew with Lentil Burgers...50
Spicy Quinoa Burgers..52
Fried Zucchini and Pepper Burgers 53
Peanut Butter Burgers...54

Table of Contents

Garlic Eggplant Burgers...55
Garlic Potato Burgers..56
Eggplant and Cauliflower Fried Burgers..57
Okra Burgers..58
Garlic Brown Rice Burgers..59
Black Bean and Lime Burgers..60
Beet and Black Bean Fried Burger...62
Minty Green Pea Burgers...63
Spicy Cilantro Burgers...64
Wheat Germ/Pumpkin Burgers..66
Almond Lentil Burgers..68
Tofu Tomato Burgers...70
Mushroom Pecan Burgers..72
Soybean Tofu Burgers..73
Paprika Pepper Burgers..74
Carrot Zucchini Burgers..75
Sweet Potato Burgers with Basil and Onion..76
Sun-dried Tomatoes and Black Bean Burgers...77
Tofu Burgers with Cayenne Pepper..78

Baked Burgers

Parsley Sweet Potato Burgers...81
Red Potato Quinoa Burgers...82
Portobello Burgers Marmalade..83
Parsley Bulgur Burgers...84
Brown Rice Carrot Burgers...85
Tofu Burgers with Corn...86
Garlic Tofu Burger...87

Veggie Burgers: 150 Delicious Vegan Burger Recipes

Black-eye Pea Burgers 88
Chickpea Artichoke Burgers 89
Sunflower Cumin Burgers 90
Millet Vegetable Burgers 91
Lentil Peanut Butter Burgers 92
Lemon Chickpea Burgers 93
Oat and Pine Nut Burgers 94
Raisin Walnut Burgers 95
Pumpkin Oat Burgers 96
Garlic Oatmeal Burgers 97
Sunflower Burgers with Garlic Sauce 98
Herbed Tofu Burgers 99
Roasted Eggplant Burgers 100
Beetroot Burgers and Barley Salad 101
Potato Bean Burgers 103
Italian Courgette Burgers 104
Cayenne Celery Burgers 105
Lentil Broccoli Burgers 106
Almond/Peanut Butter Burger 107
Coriander Mint Burgers 108
Broccoli Cauliflower Burgers 109
Quinoa Carrot Burgers 110
Cauliflower Leek Burgers 111
Bean and Garlic Burgers 112
Chickpea Soy Sauce Burgers 113
Rosemary Mushroom Burgers 114
Coriander Sunflower Seed Burgers 115

Bean Burgers

Black Bean Burgers with Sour Cream and Lime 119
Pumpkin Black Bean Burgers 121
Jalapeno Lima Bean Burgers 123
Freekeh and Harissa Burgers 125
White Burger with Tomato 127
Scallion Potato Burgers 129
Cornmeal Crusted Black Bean Burgers 131
Cilantro Bean Burger 133
Mushroom Garlic Burgers 135
Chili Powder Oat Burgers 137
Mexican Sliders 139
Chipotle Sweet Potato Burgers 141
Black Beans & Oat Burgers 143

Chickpea Burgers

Sweet Potato Cilantro Burgers with Peanut Sauce 147
Cajun Burgers 149
Curry Peanut Butter Burgers 151
Cilantro Zucchini Burgers 152

Lentils

Mushroom Lentil Burgers 157
Cumin Carrot Burger 159
Brown Rice Burgers 161

Mushroom Burgers

Mushroom with Garlic Mayonnaise 165

Potato, Portobello, Peach Burgers...167

Mushrooms Black Bean Burgers 169

Crimini Lentil Onion Burger...171

Vegetable Burgers

Hummus Eggplant Burger..175

Broccoli Scallion Burgers with Tahini 176

Spinach Burger with Vegan Cheese...178

Chili Potato Burger...180

Red Pepper Spinach Burgers 182

Burgers and Fries 184

Mixed Vegetables Burger 186

Grain, Nut and Seed Burgers

Quinoa, Chili Powder Burgers 191

Lemon Bell Pepper Burger...193

Lentil Quinoa Burgers 195

Chive Burgers 197

Tomato Spinach Burgers 199

Spicy Mustard Buckwheat Burgers..201

Walnut Rice Burgers.. 203

Nutty Oat Burger 205

Peanut Butter Oat Burgers 207

Raisin Walnut Burger... 209

Seitan

Smoky Garlic Celery Burger..213

Caper Burgers with Paprika...215

Table of Contents

Soy
Nutty Soy Burgers with Ketchup 219
Sesame Tofu Burger 221
Sauerkraut Burger 223
Gravy TVP Burgers 225

Super Combo Burgers
Barbecue Brown Rice Burger 229
Mexican Style Burgers 230
Zucchini Apple Burger 232

BONUS RECIPE
Purple Burger 234

Vegan burger buns!!

Servings	14-16 vegan burger buns

INGREDIENTS:
- 2 cups of Spelt flour
- 1 teaspoon salt
- 2 teaspoons of dry yeast
- 1/4 cup sugar
- Cup and a half of water

DIRECTIONS:
1. Knead the dough (not too much) in a mixer or by hand.
2. Cover the dough until it rises and double its size.
3. Form 16 hamburger buns from the dough and place them on a baking dish with baking paper.
4. Meanwhile, heat the oven to 240 degrees and put at the bottom of the oven a heat resistant bowl with a bit of water.
5. Bake in the oven for 18-20 minutes.
6. Wait until they get cold (if you can, the smell usually doesn't allow it...) and enjoy the delicious buns!

Lentil Oatmeal Burgers

Servings	4–6 burgers

INGREDIENTS:
- 1 1/2 cup uncooked black lentils
- 1 cup brown rice
- 1 small onion, finely chopped
- 1 carrot, peeled and finely grated
- 2 garlic cloves, minced
- 1 cup uncooked oatmeal
- Salt, pepper (to taste)
- 2 tablespoons freshly chopped parsley

DIRECTIONS:
1. Bring 5 cups of water and a pinch of salt to a boil. Add rice and allow to cook for 20 minutes, stirring occasionally. Add lentils and oatmeal and allow to cook for 20 more minutes, stirring occasionally.
2. After rice, lentils and oatmeal mixture has cooled, transfer to a large serving bowl. Add onion, carrot, and garlic to mixture and stir. Add salt and pepper, to taste. Finally, add the parsley, and with wet hands, mold the combined mixture into a burger shape.
3. In a large frying pan, add one tablespoon of olive oil. Bring the pan to desired heat and add burger mixture. Cook until golden brown. It should take approximately 5–6 minutes to cook on each side.
4. Serve with bread, your favorite burger toppings and condiments, enjoy!

White/Black Bean Burgers

Servings	8–10 burgers

INGREDIENTS:
- 2 cups canned black beans, drained
- 2 cups canned white beans, drained
- 1/3 cup uncooked oatmeal
- 1 carrot, peeled and sliced
- 2 tablespoons olive oil
- 1 teaspoon cumin powder
- 4 garlic cloves, minced 1 teaspoon onion powder
- 1/4 teaspoon cayenne pepper
- Salt, freshly ground pepper (to taste)
- 1/2 cup sesame seeds

DIRECTIONS:
1. Place oatmeal and carrots into food processor and pulse until ground. Add beans, olive oil, onion power, cumin, garlic, cayenne pepper, salt and pepper, pulse until ingredients form a paste.
2. Remove ingredients from food processor and form paste into burger shape using wet hands. Place each burger into the sesame seeds, coating each side, and set burger aside.
3. Add one tablespoon of olive oil to a frying pan. Burger will be cooked thoroughly when both sides are a golden brown.
4. Serve on your favorite bread, using toppings of your choice and tastiest condiments.

Lentil/Pea Burgers with Cayenne

Servings	6-8 burgers

INGREDIENTS:

- 3 cups canned lentils, drained
- 1 cup cooked peas
- 1 cup sweet potatoes, cooked
- 1/2 cup oatmeal
- 1 teaspoon lemon juice
- 1 teaspoon soy sauce
- 1/4 teaspoon cayenne pepper
- 1 teaspoon garlic powder
- 1 teaspoon onion powder
- Salt, pepper (to taste)

DIRECTIONS:

1. Pulse lentils and peas in food processor until ground. Place potatoes and oatmeal into food processor and pulse until a paste is formed. Put paste into mixing bowl and add lemon juice, soy sauce, cayenne pepper, garlic powder and onion powder. Combine all ingredients. Wet your hands and form mixture into burger form.

2. Add one tablespoon of olive oil to a frying pan and heat pan over medium heat. Add burgers and cook both sides until golden brown.

3. Serve on your favorite bread, with your favorite toppings and condiments.

Eggplant Pesto Burgers

Servings	4 burgers

INGREDIENTS:
- 2 small eggplants, cut into 1/2 inch thick slices
- 3 tablespoons olive oil
- 3 tablespoons balsamic vinegar
- 1 teaspoon dried basil
- 1 teaspoon dried oregano
- 4 medium size Vegan burger buns
- 4 tomato slices
- 4 lettuce leaves
- Salt, pepper

FOR THE PESTO:
- 1 cup packed basil leaves
- 1/2 cup pine nuts
- 4 tablespoons olive oil
- 1 teaspoon lemon juice

DIRECTIONS:
1. To take the bitterness out of eggplant, there is a simple process. Place the eggplant slices in a colander and sprinkle slices with an ample amount of salt. Leave the eggplant with salt in colander for thirty minutes. Rinse the eggplant and dab them dry with paper towels.
2. Heat a frying pan and one tablespoon of olive oil. Cook eggplant until it is soft, it should take approximately seven minutes on each side.

3. While your eggplant is cooking, whisk balsamic vinegar, dried basil and oregano in a medium sized mixing bowl. Once the slices are cooked, place them in mixing bowl and allow to marinade while you prepare the pesto.
4. Place basil leaves, pine nuts and lemon juice in food processor and pulse. Gradually add the olive oil and blend until smooth.
5. Allow eggplant to marinade two hours for best flavor, or serve immediately with your choice of bread, favorite toppings, and pesto.

Cauliflower Burgers with Curry

Servings	4–6 burgers

INGREDIENTS:
- 1 head cauliflower, cut into florets
- 1 teaspoon curry
- 2 tablespoons tahini paste
- 1/2 cup breadcrumbs
- 2 tablespoons chopped chives
- 2 tablespoons sunflower seeds
- Salt, pepper (to taste)

DIRECTIONS:

1. Steam cauliflower florets approximately 20 minutes, until tender. Mash cooked florets in mixing bowl using a potato masher. Add tahini paste, curry, breadcrumbs, chopped chives, and sunflower seeds. Mix ingredients until well blended. Form mixture into burger shape.

2. Add one tablespoon olive oil to frying pan. Cook burgers until slightly brown on both sides, about 7 minutes for each side.

3. Serve on your choice of bun, favorite toppings and condiments.

Black Bean Mushroom Burgers

Servings	8–10 burgers

INGREDIENTS:
- 3 cups canned black beans, drained and rinsed
- 1 cup mushrooms, diced
- 2/3 cup rolled oats
- 3 garlic cloves
- 1 teaspoon cumin seeds
- 4 tablespoons sesame seeds
- 2 tablespoons vegetable oil
- Salt, pepper (to taste)

DIRECTIONS:
1. Puree one and half cans of the black beans in a food processor with mushrooms, garlic, cumin seeds, salt and pepper until smooth. Put puree mixture into a large mixing bowl. Add remaining black beans and rolled oats, stir.
2. Using wet hands, form mixture into burger shape. Coat burger on each side with sesame seeds.
3. Add one tablespoon of the vegetable oil to a frying pan and set burner to medium heat. Cook both sides of burger until browned at the edge, approximately seven minutes for each side.
4. Serve with your favorite roll, toppings, and condiment.

Powerful Green Burgers

Servings	4-6 burgers

INGREDIENTS:
- 1 broccoli head, cut into florets
- 1 cup canned cooked green peas
- 1 teaspoon cumin powder
- 1/2 teaspoon garlic powder
- Salt, pepper (to taste)

DIRECTIONS:
1. Steam broccoli until tender, approximately 15-20 minutes. Allow to cool.
2. Add entire ingredient list to a food processor and pulse until a paste is formed. Wet hands and form paste from processor into a burger shape.
3. Heat one tablespoon of olive oil over medium heat. Cook both sides of burger until color is a golden brown.
4. Serve with your favorite bread, toppings and condiments.

Portobello Burgers with Balsamic Vinegar

Servings	2 burgers

INGREDIENTS:

- 2 Portobello mushrooms
- 2 tablespoons balsamic vinegar
- 2 tablespoons chopped parsley
- Salt, pepper (to taste)

DIRECTIONS:

1. Add one tablespoon olive oil to a frying pan. Heat pan over medium heat. Place mushrooms in pan and salt and pepper to taste. Cook on each side for five minutes.

2. Remove the mushrooms from heat and place in a small mixing bowl, add remaining ingredients and toss mushrooms to evenly coat.

3. Serve mixture on your favorite bread, toppings, and condiments.

Cayenne Chickpea Burgers

Servings	4–6 burgers

INGREDIENTS:
- 2 cups canned chickpeas
- 3 garlic cloves, minced
- 2 tablespoons olive oil
- 1 teaspoon cumin
- 1 teaspoon curry powder
- 1/4 teaspoon cayenne pepper
- 1 tablespoon rice flour
- 2 tablespoons chopped coriander
- Salt, pepper (to taste)

DIRECTIONS:

1. Pulse chickpeas in food processor until they form a paste. Add garlic, curry powder, cumin, coriander and cayenne to paste and mix well. Wet your hands and form mixture into burger shape.

2. Add one tablespoon of olive oil to frying pan and heat pan over medium heat. Cook burgers on each side for ten minutes, flipping after five minutes.

3. Serve with your favorite bun and add this sauce to give your burger superb flavor. Mix 1/2 cup almond yogurt with 2 tablespoons freshly chopped dill. Spread evenly over burgers.

Potato Burgers

Servings	4-6 burgers

INGREDIENTS:
- 1 1/2 cup canned white beans
- 1 small carrot, grated
- 1 green onion, finely chopped
- 4 potatoes, grated
- 1/2 cup corn
- Salt, pepper (to taste)
- 2 tablespoons fresh parsley

DIRECTIONS:
1. Puree beans in a blender until a smooth paste. In a large mixing bowl, combine paste with remaining ingredients.
2. Form the mixture into burger shape using wet hands. Cook in a frying pan over medium heat for 7 minutes on each side. Use one tablespoon of olive oil in pan to prevent sticking.
3. Serve on your favorite bun with your favorite garlic sauce to add robust flavor.

Bean Mushroom Burgers

Servings	4–6 burgers

INGREDIENTS:
- 1 1/2 cup fresh chopped mushrooms
- 2 garlic cloves, minced
- 1 cup canned white beans
- 1 tablespoon chopped parsley
- 2 green onions, chopped
- 1/4 teaspoon cumin powder
- Salt, pepper (to taste)

DIRECTIONS:
1. Puree the beans in a small blender. Place the puree into a medium sized mixing bowl and combine with the remaining ingredients.
2. Using wet hands, form the mixture into a burger shape.
3. Add one tablespoon of olive oil to frying pan and heat over medium. Cook burgers on each side 8 minutes, until golden brown.

Kidney Bean Burgers with Pumpkin Seeds

Servings	8–10 burgers

INGREDIENTS:
- 3 cups canned kidney beans
- 3/4 cup rolled oats
- 1/2 teaspoon tamarind paste
- 2 garlic cloves, minced
- 1/2 small onion, chopped
- 1 cup baby spinach leaves, chopped
- 1 teaspoon nutritional yeast
- 1/2 cup pumpkin seeds
- 1/4 teaspoon chili powder
- Salt, pepper (to taste)

DIRECTIONS:
1. Form a paste in a food processor with the kidney beans, use pulse setting. Combine paste and the rest of ingredient list in a large mixing bowl and mix.
2. Using wet hands, form the mixture into a burger shape.
3. Add one tablespoon of olive oil to frying pan and heat over medium. Cook burgers on each side 7 minutes, until heated through.

Eggplant Tomato Burgers

Servings	4 burgers

INGREDIENTS:
- 1 eggplant, sliced
- 2 large tomato, cut in thick slices
- 2 tablespoons balsamic vinegar
- 2 tablespoons olive oil
- 1/2 teaspoon dried basil
- Salt, pepper

DIRECTIONS:
1. To take the bitterness out of eggplant, there is a simple process. Place the eggplant slices in a colander and sprinkle slices with an ample amount of salt. Leave the eggplant with salt in colander for thirty minutes. Rinse the eggplant and dab them dry with paper towels.
2. Combine balsamic vinegar with olive oil and coat eggplant on each side with mixture.
3. Add one tablespoon of olive oil to frying pan and heat over medium. Cook eggplant slices on each side 3-5 minutes, until tender. Replace eggplant in pan with tomato slices and repeat.
4. Serve with the vegan bun listed in the beginning of this cookbook.

Mushroom Burgers

Servings	2 burgers

INGREDIENTS:
- 2 large Portobello mushrooms
- 1/4 cup balsamic vinegar
- 2 tablespoons extra virgin olive oil
- 1 garlic clove, minced
- 1 teaspoon dried basil
- Salt, pepper (to taste)

DIRECTIONS:
1. Combine entire list of ingredients and allow to marinate for approximately 30 minutes for best flavor.
2. Add one tablespoon of olive oil to frying pan and heat over medium. Mushroom will only take about 3 minutes to cook on each side.
3. Serve over your favorite bread choice.

Black Bean/Broccoli Burgers

Servings	4–6 burgers

INGREDIENTS:
- 1 1/2 cups canned black beans
- 1 red bell pepper, cored and chopped
- 2 green onions
- 1/2 cup wheat germ
- 2 garlic cloves, minced
- 1/2 cup pumpkin seeds
- 1 teaspoon nutritional yeast
- 1/4 teaspoon cayenne pepper
- 1 teaspoon dried basil
- 1/2 teaspoon dried oregano
- Salt, pepper (to taste)

DIRECTIONS:
1. Puree beans in a small blender until a paste forms. In a separate bowl, add paste, onions and red pepper, combine.
2. Grind pumpkin seeds and garlic in food processor. Combine the ground ingredients with the rest of the ingredients list and mix together with paste mixture.
3. Using wet hands, form the mixture into a burger shape.
4. Add one tablespoon of olive oil to frying pan and heat over medium. Cook burgers on each side 7 minutes, until golden brown.
5. Serve with your choice of bread, toppings, and condiments.

Zucchini Balsamic Vinegar Burgers

Servings	4–6 burgers

INGREDIENTS:
- 1 zucchini, cut in 1/4 inch thick slices
- 2 tablespoons olive oil
- 1 tablespoon balsamic vinegar
- Salt, pepper

DIRECTIONS:

1. To take the bitterness out of zucchini, there is a simple process. Place the zucchini slices in a colander and sprinkle slices with an ample amount of salt. Leave the zucchini with salt in colander for thirty minutes. Rinse the zucchini and dab them dry with paper towels. Place in mixing bowl, drizzle olive oil over slices and toss until evenly coated.

2. Add one tablespoon of olive oil to frying pan and heat over medium. Cook burgers on each side 4 minutes, until golden in color. Remove from heat and soak in balsamic vinegar, salt and pepper.

3. Serve delicious slices over your favorite choice of bread and toppings.

Sweet Potato and Bean Burgers

Servings	8-10 burgers

INGREDIENTS:
- 3 cups cannellini white beans, drained
- 2 sweet potatoes, peeled, boiled and mashed
- 3 tablespoons tahini paste
- 1 teaspoon Cajun seasoning
- 1/3 cup whole wheat flour
- Salt, pepper to taste

DIRECTIONS:
1. Puree the beans in a food processor until smooth. In a large mixing bowl combine beans with mashed potatoes and stir. Add the rest of the ingredient list and mix well.
2. Using wet hands, form the mixture into a burger shape.
3. Add one tablespoon of olive oil to frying pan and heat over medium. Cook burgers on each side 4 minutes, until golden brown.
4. Serve with your choice of bread, toppings, and condiments.

Tofu Portobello Burgers

Servings	4 burgers

INGREDIENTS:
- 4 Portobello mushrooms
- 1 large red onion, sliced
- 1 tablespoon balsamic vinegar
- 2 garlic cloves, minced
- 2 tablespoons olive oil
- 10 oz firm packed tofu
- 1/2 cup red wine
- 1 tablespoon soy sauce
- 1 teaspoon agave syrup
- 1 tablespoon sesame seeds

DIRECTIONS:
1. In a medium mixing bowl, whisk together the four ingredients below the tofu in the list, include a dash of freshly ground pepper. Slice the tofu and place in mixture for thirty minutes to infuse with flavor.
2. Prepare the portabellas for cooking by slicing and removing stems. Fry the mushrooms over medium heat until cooked through.
3. Remove mushrooms and place tofu in same pan. Cook until browned.
4. Mix together the remaining ingredients. Layer ingredients and marinade over bread and serve.

Mushroom Pineapple Burgers

Servings	2 burgers

INGREDIENTS:
- 2 Portobello mushrooms
- 2 slices fresh pineapple
- 1/4 cup teriyaki sauce
- 1 teaspoon agave syrup
- Salt, pepper
- Vegan burger buns

DIRECTIONS:
1. Create a sauce by combining teriyaki sauce, agave syrup, and salt/pepper. Brush the sauce over mushrooms and pineapple, coating evenly.
2. Add one tablespoon of olive oil to frying pan and heat over medium. Cook mushrooms on each side 7 minutes, until golden brown. Heat pineapple in pan with mushrooms until cooked through.
3. Using the vegan burger bun for serving, layer mushrooms and pineapple and enjoy!

Chickpeas Burgers

Servings	6–8 burgers

INGREDIENTS:
- 3 oz bulgur
- 2 cups water
- 1 1/2 cups canned chickpeas
- 1/2 cup fresh chopped parsley
- 1 tablespoon all purpose flour
- 2 garlic cloves, minced
- 2 tablespoons breadcrumbs
- 1 tablespoon olive oil
- Salt, pepper (to taste)

DIRECTIONS:
1. Bring 2 cups water to a boil. Add bulgur and cook until water has been absorbed, let cool.
2. Create a paste with the chickpeas by placing in food processor and pulsing. Add the paste and remaining ingredient list to the bulgur and combine.
3. Using wet hands, form the mixture into a burger shape.
4. Add one tablespoon of olive oil to frying pan and heat over medium. Cook burgers on each side approximately 5 minutes, until golden brown.

Quinoa Pepper Burgers

Servings	6–8 burgers

INGREDIENTS:
- 2/3 cup uncooked quinoa
- 3 cups water or vegetable broth
- 4 roasted red bell peppers
- 1 cup canned white beans
- 2 tablespoons chopped coriander
- Salt, pepper (to taste)

DIRECTIONS:

1. Bring 3 cups water/broth to a boil. Add quinoa, remove from heat and allow quinoa to absorb all of the liquid.

2. Combine the bell pepper and beans in food processor and pulse until a paste forms. In a medium mixing bowl, combine paste, quinoa, coriander, and salt/pepper.

3. Using wet hands, form the mixture into a burger shape.

4. Add one tablespoon of olive oil to frying pan and heat over medium. Cook burgers on each side 7 minutes, until crispy.

Portobello Onion Burgers

Servings	2 burgers

INGREDIENTS:
- 1 large green onion, cut into rings
- 2 tablespoons olive oil
- 2 Portobello mushrooms
- 1 teaspoon balsamic vinegar
- 1/8 teaspoon chili flakes
- 1 teaspoon agave syrup
- 1 teaspoon soy sauce
- Salt, pepper (to taste)

DIRECTIONS:

1. Add one tablespoon of olive oil to frying pan and heat over low. Sauté onions for approximately 20 minutes, until tender. After cooked, add chili flakes.

2. In a large mixing bowl, create a sauce by combining soy sauce, balsamic vinegar, agave syrup, and salt/pepper. Coat the mushrooms evenly with this sauce.

3. Add one tablespoon of olive oil to frying pan and heat over medium. Cook burgers on each side 7 minutes, until golden brown.

Tropical Island Burgers

Servings	6–8 burgers

INGREDIENTS:
- 3 cups canned black beans, rinsed and drained
- 1/2 cup rolled oats
- 4 tablespoons sweet corn
- 1/4 cup crushed pineapple
- 1 teaspoon mustard
- Salt, pepper (to taste)

DIRECTIONS:
1. Create a paste with beans and oats by pulsing in food processor. In a large mixing bowl, combine paste with remaining ingredient list.
2. Using wet hands, form the mixture into a burger shape.
3. Add one tablespoon of olive oil to frying pan and heat over medium. Cook burgers on each side 7 minutes, until brown and crispy.

Tofu Almond Burgers

Servings	6–8 burgers

INGREDIENTS:
- 2 tablespoons flax seeds, freshly ground
- 4 tablespoons water
- 1 package firm tofu, crumbled
- 1 carrot, peeled and grated
- 2 green onions, finely chopped
- 2 tablespoons sesame oil
- 1 teaspoon grated ginger
- 2 garlic cloves, minced
- 2/3 cup slivered almonds, toasted
- 2 teaspoons soy sauce
- 1 tablespoon sesame seeds

DIRECTIONS:
1. In a small mixing bowl, combine flax seed and water.
1. Pour sesame oil in a large skillet and warm on low heat. Sauté green onion, carrot, garlic and ginger for 4–5 minutes, until tender. In a large mixing bowl, add remaining ingredient list, flax seed mixture, sautéed items and combine.
1. Using wet hands, form the mixture into a burger shape.
1. Add one tablespoon of olive oil to frying pan and heat over medium. Cook burgers on each side 6 minutes, until golden brown.

Mushroom Broccoli Burgers

Servings	6–8 burgers

INGREDIENTS:
- 1 small red onion, finely chopped
- 2 garlic cloves, minced
- 2 tablespoons olive oil
- 2 cups chopped mushrooms
- 1 cup cooked quinoa
- 1 1/2 cup canned pinto beans
- 2 carrots, peeled and sliced
- 1/2 head of broccoli, cut into florets
- 1/2 teaspoon cumin seeds
- Salt, pepper (to taste)
- 2 tablespoons chopped coriander leaves

DIRECTIONS:
1. Sauté onion and garlic in large skillet with olive oil for 2 minutes. Add prepared mushrooms and cook until tender and water has evaporated.
1. Steam carrots and broccoli together, approximately 10 minutes until tender. Coarsely mash in large mixing bowl. Add sautéed items to mixing bowl and also remaining ingredient list and mix well.
1. Using wet hands, form the mixture into a burger shape.
1. Add one tablespoon of olive oil to frying pan and heat over medium. Cook burgers on each side 5 minutes, until crispy.
1. Serve with favorite bun, toppings, and condiments.

Sweet Corn/Potato Burgers

Servings	8-10 burgers

INGREDIENTS:
- 2 pounds sweet potatoes, peeled and cubed
- 2 tablespoons olive oil
- 1 onion, finely chopped
- 1 green chili, chopped
- 1 teaspoon dried coriander
- 2 cups canned sweet corn
- 1 cup cornmeal
- 2 tablespoons packed parsley leaves, chopped
- Salt, pepper (to taste)

DIRECTIONS:
1. Preheat oven to 375 degrees. Place cubed sweet potatoes in baking dish. Season with salt/pepper and drizzle with oil. Cover with aluminum foil and bake 40 minutes. Potatoes will be done when their edges are golden brown.
2. Once cooked, put in large mixing bowl and mash. Stir in remaining ingredients from list and mix well.
3. Using wet hands, form the mixture into a burger shape.
4. Add one tablespoon of olive oil to frying pan and heat over medium. Cook burgers on each side 7 minutes, until golden brown.
5. Serve with the vegan burger, your favorite vegetables, and condiments.

Spicy Thai Burger

Servings	10–12 burgers

INGREDIENTS:
- 4 cups canned white beans
- 1 cup rolled oats
- 1 teaspoon cumin
- 1 teaspoon fresh ginger, grated
- 2 garlic cloves, minced
- 1 teaspoon turmeric
- 1 carrot, peeled and grated
- 4 cherry tomatoes, quartered
- 2 green onions, chopped
- 2 tablespoons fresh Thai basil, chopped
- 1/4 cup unsweetened coconut milk
- 1 teaspoon lime juice
- 1 red pepper, deseeded and sliced
- 2 tablespoons vegetable oil
- Salt, pepper

DIRECTIONS:
1. Create paste using beans, garlic, ginger and turmeric in a food processor on pulse setting. Add paste to large mixing bowl with rolled oats and mix well.
2. Using wet hands, form the mixture into a burger shape.
3. Add one tablespoon of olive oil to frying pan and heat over medium. Cook burgers on each side 6 minutes, until golden brown.
4. Make a vegetable garnish, by combining carrots, tomatoes, chopped basil and green onions in a medium mixing bowl.

5. In small mixing bowl, whisk to combine coconut milk, lime juice and red pepper. Poor milk mixture over the vegetable garnish and coat evenly.
6. Place the burger on your roll of choice and a spoonful of the vegetable garnish.

Summer Squash Burgers

Servings	6–8 burgers

INGREDIENTS:
- 1 yellow squash, chopped
- 1 zucchini, chopped
- 1 1/2 cups cooked brown rice
- 1 cup breadcrumbs
- 3 tablespoons tomato puree
- 1 tablespoon flax seeds, ground
- 3 tablespoons water
- Salt, pepper (to taste)

DIRECTIONS:
1. Combine flax seeds and water in small bowl.
2. Combine rest of ingredients in large mixing bowl and mix with flax seed mixture.
3. Using wet hands, form the mixture into a burger shape.
4. Add one tablespoon of olive oil to frying pan and heat over medium. Cook burgers on each side 7 minutes, until crispy brown.
5. Serve with favorite roll and toppings.

Pineapple Buckwheat Burgers

Servings	6-8 burgers

INGREDIENTS:
- 2 1/2 cup canned beans of choice, drained and rinsed
- 1/2 cup buckwheat
- 1 onion, chopped
- 2 garlic cloves
- 1/2 teaspoon chili powder
- 1 teaspoon cumin
- 1 teaspoon dried oregano
- 2 tablespoons olive oil
- 1 fresh pineapple, cut into thin slices
- Salt, pepper (to taste)

DIRECTIONS:
1. Bring one cup of water to a boil. Add buckwheat and cook approximately 10-15 minutes, until all liquid has been absorbed.
2. Place all remaining ingredients, minus the pineapple slices into food processor and pulse until a paste is formed. Combine paste and buckwheat.
3. Using wet hands, form the mixture into a burger shape.
4. Add one tablespoon of olive oil to frying pan and heat over medium. Cook burgers on each side 6 minutes, they will be a nice brown color. Grill the pineapple as well.
5. Serve the patties layered with pineapple with your bun of choice.

Broccoli Leak Burgers

Servings	4–6 burgers

INGREDIENTS:
- 1 head broccoli, trimmed and cut into florets
- 2 leeks, finely chopped (only the white part)
- 1 tablespoon flax seeds, ground
- 2 tablespoons water
- 2 potatoes, peeled and cubed
- 3 tablespoons olive oil
- 1 teaspoon dried thyme
- Salt, pepper (to taste)

DIRECTIONS:
1. Combine flax seed and water in small mixing bowl and allow to soak.
2. Steam broccoli and potato together until tender, approximately 20 minutes, mash.
3. In a skillet, sauté onions with olive oil until translucent
4. Combine all mixtures and remaining ingredients in large mixing bowl.
5. Using wet hands, form the mixture into a burger shape.
6. Add one tablespoon of olive oil to frying pan and heat over medium. Cook burgers on each side 6 minutes, until golden brown.

Soybean Burgers

Servings	6–8 burgers

INGREDIENTS:
- 3 cups canned soybeans, drained
- 1/2 cup sunflower seeds
- 1/2 cup pecans
- 1/2 teaspoon cayenne pepper
- 1 carrot, peeled and grated
- 2 garlic cloves, minced
- 1 celery stalk, finely chopped
- 2 cups rolled oats
- Salt, pepper (to taste)

DIRECTIONS:

1. Add soybeans, sunflower seeds, pecans, cayenne pepper and a pinch of salt to a food processor and pulse until smooth. Add mixture to large mixing bowl.
2. Add carrot, garlic and celery, and rolled oats to large mixing bowl with mixture and combine.
3. Using wet hands, form the mixture into a burger shape.
4. Add one tablespoon of olive oil to frying pan and heat over medium. Cook burgers on each side 6 minutes, until crispy.
5. Serve with vegan roll and favorite condiments.

Tofu Marmalade Burgers

Servings	2 burgers

INGREDIENTS:
- 2 tofu slices
- 1 tablespoon soy sauce
- 1 tablespoon agave syrup
- 1 tablespoon lemon juice
- 3 red onions, sliced
- 1/4 cup red wine
- 2 tablespoons rice vinegar
- 5 tablespoons brown sugar
- 1 star anise
- Salt, pepper (to taste)

DIRECTIONS:
1. Place soy sauce, agave syrup and lemon juice in a large mixing bowl and stir. Put tofu slices in bowl and evenly coat. Cook tofu in frying pan over medium heat, 4-5 minutes on each side.
2. Put remaining ingredients into a sauce pan and combine. Bring to a boil over medium heat and then heat down to low and cook for 15-20 minutes, until all items are tender.
3. Put spoonful of marmalade over tofu slices and serve.

Spinach and Pistachio Burgers

Servings	6–8 burgers

INGREDIENTS:

- 3 cups spinach leaves
- 1 green onion, chopped
- 2 cups canned white beans
- 2/3 cup pistachio, ground
- 1 cup rolled oats
- 1 teaspoon cumin
- 1 teaspoon soy sauce
- Salt, pepper

DIRECTIONS:

1. Steam spinach for 2 minutes. Finely chop the spinach after steaming and put into large mixing bowl.
2. Pulse the beans using a food processor until a paste forms. Add paste to spinach. Add remaining list of ingredients and wet hands to form mixture in a burger shape.
3. Add one tablespoon of olive oil to a frying pan and cook burger on medium heat, approximately 5 minutes on each side, until golden brown.

Fried Burgers

Pinto Burgers with Chipotle Aioli

Servings	6–8 burgers

INGREDIENTS:

For burgers:
- 2 cups canned pinto beans, drained and rinsed
- 1 red onion, finely chopped
- 1 red pepper, finely chopped
- 1/2 cup sweet corn, fresh or frozen
- 2 tablespoons vegetable oil
- 2 garlic cloves, minced
- 1 teaspoon cumin powder
- 1/2 teaspoon dried oregano
- 2 tablespoons tomato puree
- Salt, pepper (to taste)
- 1/4 cup cornmeal

For the chipotle aioli:
- 1/2 cup coconut yogurt
- 1 chipotle in adobo sauce, finely chopped
- 1 tablespoon adobo sauce
- 1 garlic clove, minced
- 1 pinch of salt

DIRECTIONS:

To make the burgers:
1. Coarsely mash the beans with a potato masher in a large mixing bowl.

2. Add olive oil to large frying pan, sauté the onion until translucent. Add garlic, pepper and corn, cook mixture five minutes. Add contents of frying pan to large mixing bowl with the beans. Add the remaining ingredient list and mix well. Wet hands to shape mixture into a patty form.
3. Add one tablespoon of olive oil to frying pan and over medium heat, cook the burgers, 5 minutes each side, until browned.

To make the aioli:

1. Combine coconut yogurt with the chopped chipotle, adobo sauce, garlic and a pinch of salt in a small mixing bowl.

Fried Burgers

Fennel and Beetroot Burger

Servings	6–8 burgers

INGREDIENTS:
- 2 medium size beetroots, peeled and grated
- 2 tablespoons chopped dill
- 1 fennel bulb, trimmed and finely chopped
- 1 cup cooked brown rice
- 2 tablespoons cornmeal
- 1/4 cup tomato sauce
- Salt, pepper (tp taste)

DIRECTIONS:
1. In a large mixing bowl, combine grated beets, fennel, dill, brown rice and cornmeal. Stir in the tomato sauce, salt/pepper, form small patties.
2. Add one tablespoon of olive oil to frying pan and fry burger for 6 minutes on each side.
3. Serve on vegan burger buns and favorite toppings.

Mushroom Chickpea Burgers

Servings	6–8 burgers

INGREDIENTS:
- 2 cups mushrooms, finely chopped
- 1 onion, chopped
- 2 garlic cloves, minced
- 1 teaspoon curry powder
- 1 cup canned chickpeas, drained
- 2 carrots, peeled and grated
- 2 tablespoons chopped coriander
- 2 tablespoons flour
- Salt, pepper (to taste)

DIRECTIONS:
1. In a medium size frying pan, heat one tablespoon of olive oil and sauté onion and garlic for approximately 2 minutes. Add curry, carrots and mushrooms, turn heat down to low and continue to cook for ten minutes. Set aside.
2. In a food processor, pulse the chickpeas until a paste forms. In a large mixing bowl, combine the mushroom mixture an the paste. Stir in coriander, flour, and salt/pepper.
3. Wet your hands and mold mixture into a burger shape.
4. Add one tablespoon of olive oil to a frying pan on medium heat. Burger will be cooked thoroughly when both sides are a golden brown.
5. Serve on your favorite bread, using toppings of your choice and tastiest condiments.

Fried Burgers

Sweet Corn Burgers with Chickpea

Servings	6–8 burgers

INGREDIENTS:
- 1 1/3 cups fresh or frozen sweet corn
- 1 1/2 cup canned chickpeas, drained and rinsed
- 2 tablespoons flax seeds, ground
- 6 tablespoons water
- 1/4 cup cornmeal
- 1/2 cup all purpose whole wheat flour
- 1 teaspoon baking powder
- 1/4 cup chopped green onions
- Salt, pepper (to taste)

DIRECTIONS:
1. In a small mixing bowl, combine the flax seed and water and allow to set for ten minutes.
2. In a food processor, pulse the chickpeas until a small paste forms. In a large mixing bowl, put the paste, the flax seed mixture and the remaining of the dry ingredients listed, combine ingredients by mixing.
3. Wet your hands and mold mixture into a burger shape.
4. Add one tablespoon of olive oil to a frying pan on medium heat. Burger will be cooked thoroughly when both sides are a golden brown.
5. Serve on your favorite bread, using toppings of your choice and tastiest condiments.

Fried Potato and Garlic Burgers

Servings: 6–8 burgers

INGREDIENTS:
- 2 pounds potatoes, peeled and cubed
- 3 garlic cloves, minced
- 1/2 cup flour, plus more for coating
- 2 tablespoons fresh chopped dill
- salt, pepper (to taste)

DIRECTIONS:

1. Boil potatoes as you normally would and mash them when cooked.
2. Stir in everything but the flour and mix well. Finally, put the flour in and combine.
3. Wet your hands and mold mixture into a burger shape.
4. Add one tablespoon of olive oil to a frying pan on medium heat. Burger will be cooked thoroughly when both sides are a golden brown.
5. Serve on your favorite bread, using toppings of your choice and tastiest condiments.

Spicy Nut and Seed Burgers

Servings	4-6 burgers

INGREDIENTS:
- 1/3 cup pistachio, shelled and slightly toasted
- 3 cups broccoli florets
- 1/4 teaspoon chili flakes
- 1/3 cup rolled oats
- 2 tablespoons pumpkin seeds
- 2 tablespoons sunflower seeds
- 2 tablespoons black sesame
- Salt, pepper (to taste)

DIRECTIONS:

1. Steam broccoli for 10-15 minutes until tender. Pulse broccoli, pistachio and chili flakes in food processor until the mixture sticks together.

2. In a large mixing bowl, combine the broccoli mixture with the rest of the ingredient list.

3. Wet your hands and mold mixture into a burger shape.

4. Add one tablespoon of olive oil to a frying pan on medium heat. Burger will need to be cooked 5-6 minutes on each side, until a nice brown color is seen.

5. Serve on your favorite bread, using toppings of your choice and tastiest condiments.

Quinoa Beet Burgers

Servings	6-8 burgers

INGREDIENTS:
- 1 small onion, finely chopped
- 1 tablespoon olive oil
- 1 medium size beet, peeled and grated
- 2 cups baby spinach leaves
- 1 1/2 cup canned black beans, drained and rinsed
- 1 1/2 cup cooked quinoa
- 1/4 cup rolled oats
- 1 teaspoon sugar
- 1 teaspoon chopped rosemary
- Salt, pepper (to taste)

DIRECTIONS:
1. Sauté onion for 4 minutes in large frying pan with olive oil. Add spinach and beet to the frying pan and cook for 5 minutes. Once mixture is cooled, put in a large mixing bowl.
2. Puree black beans in a food processor until paste forms. Add paste and the remaining ingredients on the list to the large mixing bowl and combine.
3. Wet your hands and mold mixture into a burger shape.
4. Add one tablespoon of olive oil to a frying pan on medium heat. Burger will need to be cooked 5-6 minutes on each side, until a nice brown color is seen.
5. Serve on your favorite bread, using toppings of your choice and tastiest condiments.

Fried Burgers

Spicy Black Bean Burgers

Servings	8-10 burgers

INGREDIENTS:
- 3 cups canned black beans
- 1 small onion, finely chopped
- 2 garlic cloves
- 2 tablespoons chipotle in adobo
- 1 teaspoon cumin powder
- 2 tablespoons cornstarch
- 2 tablespoons chopped coriander
- 1/2 cups rolled oats
- 4 tablespoons olive oil
- Salt, pepper (to taste)

DIRECTIONS:
1. In a food processor, combine onion, garlic and black beans until a paste forms. Add to the food processor, chipotle, cumin powder, coriander, cornstarch and a pinch of salt. Pulse to mix well and add mixture to a large mixing bowl. Add rolled oats to the bowl and combine.
2. Wet your hands and mold mixture into a burger shape.
3. Add one tablespoon of olive oil to a frying pan on medium heat. Burger will need to be cooked 5-6 minutes on each side, until crispy around the edges.
4. Serve on your vegan roll, using toppings of your choice and tastiest condiments.

Carrot Quinoa Burgers

Servings	4–6 burgers

INGREDIENTS:
- 2 carrots, peeled and grated
- 1 parsnip, peeled and grated
- 1 1/2 cups cooked quinoa
- 1 cup canned white beans
- 2 tablespoons rice flour
- Salt, pepper (to taste)

DIRECTIONS:
1. In a food processor, pulse the beans until a paste forms. Put paste into large mixing bowl and add remaining ingredient list.
2. Wet your hands and mold mixture into a burger shape.
3. Add one tablespoon of olive oil to a frying pan on medium heat. Burger will need to be cooked 5–6 minutes on each side, until golden brown.
4. Serve on your vegan roll, using toppings of your choice and tastiest condiments.

Spicy Chickpea Oat Burgers

Servings	6-8 burgers

INGREDIENTS:
- 1/4 cup rolled oats
- 3 cups canned chickpeas, drained
- 2 garlic cloves
- 1 teaspoon curry powder
- 2 tablespoons chopped coriander
- 3 tablespoons olive oil
- Salt, pepper (to taste)

DIRECTIONS:

1. In a food processor, pulse chickpeas and oats until smooth. Add to the processor, garlic cloves, curry and coriander. Pulse to combine and add mixture to a medium mixing bowl, salt and pepper.

2. Wet your hands and mold mixture into a burger shape.

3. Add one tablespoon of olive oil to a frying pan on medium heat. Burger will need to be cooked 5-6 minutes on each side, until golden brown and crispy. If greasy, dab with paper towels to dry.

4. Serve on your vegan roll, using toppings of your choice and favorite condiments.

Cashew with Lentil Burgers

Servings	8-10 burgers

INGREDIENTS:
- 1 3/4 cups canned chickpeas, rinsed and drained
- 2 1/2 cups canned lentils, rinsed and drained
- 1/2 cup cashew pieces
- 2 carrots, peeled and grated
- 3 garlic cloves, minced
- 1 green onion, chopped
- 2 tablespoon olive oil
- 1 teaspoon curry powder
- 1 teaspoon turmeric powder
- 4 tablespoons flour
- 2 cups breadcrumbs
- 3 tablespoons olive oil
- Salt, pepper (to taste)

DIRECTIONS:
1. In a large frying pan, sauté onions and garlic until onion is translucent. Stir in the carrots, and cook until desired tenderness. Place mixture in a large mixing bowl and combine with lentils, curry powder, and turmeric.
2. Put the chickpeas and cashew nuts in a food processor and pulse a few times until a smooth paste forms. Combine paste with the vegetable mix then add the flour and salt/pepper. Coat burgers with breadcrumbs.
3. Wet your hands and mold mixture into a burger shape.

Fried Burgers

4. Add one tablespoon of olive oil to a frying pan on medium heat. Burger will need to be cooked 5–6 minutes on each side, until golden brown and crispy. If greasy, dab with paper towels to dry.
5. Serve on your vegan roll, using toppings of your choice and favorite condiments.

Spicy Quinoa Burgers

Servings	6–8 burgers

INGREDIENTS:

- 1 small onion, chopped
- 1 green pepper, deseeded and chopped
- 2 garlic cloves, minced
- 1 cup canned black beans
- 1 cup cooked quinoa
- 1 teaspoon taco seasoning
- 2 tablespoons flax seeds
- 1/2 cup breadcrumbs
- 2 tablespoons all purpose flour
- Salt, pepper (to taste)

DIRECTIONS:

1. Add 6 tablespoons of water to flax seed in small mixing bowl and let soak.
2. Sauté onions and garlic in medium frying pan with one tablespoon of olive oil for approximately 4 minutes, until onions are translucent. Allow to cool and put in a large mixing bowl.
3. In a food processor, pulse half of the quinoa and all of the beans until smooth. Place mixture in large mixing bowl with the onions and garlic, and add remaining quinoa, taco seasoning and green pepper. Combine well and add flour, breadcrumbs, and flax seed mixture.
4. Wet your hands and mold mixture into a burger shape.
5. Add one tablespoon of olive oil to a frying pan on medium heat. Burger will need to be cooked 5-6 minutes on each side, until golden brown and crispy.

Fried Zucchini and Pepper Burgers

Servings	6-8 burgers

INGREDIENTS:
- 4 oz bread, cubed
- 2 tablespoons flax seeds
- 1 red bell pepper, cored and chopped
- 1 zucchini, grated
- 2 tablespoons chives, chopped
- 1 garlic clove, minced
- 3 tablespoons flour
- Salt, pepper (to taste)

DIRECTIONS:
1. Mix the flax seeds with 2 tablespoons of water and allow them to soak.
2. Put bread crumbs in large mixing bowl and cover with water. After two or three minutes, squeeze water off from bread. Add flax seed and remaining recipe ingredients and mix well.
3. Wet your hands and mold mixture into a burger shape.
4. Add one tablespoon of olive oil to a frying pan on medium heat. Burger will need to be cooked 5-6 minutes on each side, until golden brown.
5. Serve on your choice of bread, using toppings of your choice and favorite condiments.

Peanut Butter Burgers

Servings	6–8 burgers

INGREDIENTS:
- 2 cups canned chickpeas
- 3 tablespoons peanut butter
- 1 teaspoon lemon juice
- 1 teaspoon soy sauce
- 1 teaspoon fresh grated ginger
- 1 green onion, chopped
- 1/4 teaspoon chili flakes
- 3 tablespoons coconut oil
- Salt, pepper (to taste)

DIRECTIONS:
1. Grind the chickpeas in a food processor or blender. Add peanut butter, soy sauce, lemon juice and ginger to food processor and create a smooth paste on pulse setting. Put paste mixture in a large mixing bowl and combine with green onion, chili flakes, and salt/pepper.

2. Wet your hands and mold mixture into a burger shape. Add coconut oil to a frying pan on medium heat. Burger will need to be cooked 5–6 minutes on each side, until golden brown and crispy around the edges.

Fried Burgers

Garlic Eggplant Burgers

Servings	4–6 burgers

INGREDIENTS:

- 2 large eggplant
- 1 red onion, finely chopped
- 2 garlic cloves
- 1 cup breadcrumbs
- 1 teaspoon cumin seeds
- 1 tablespoon chopped parsley
- 1 teaspoon chopped fresh mint
- Salt, pepper (to taste)

DIRECTIONS:

1. Preheat oven to 450 degrees. Prepare eggplant by cutting in half, generously sprinkling with salt/pepper and placing on a baking sheet. Bake the eggplant approximately 30–40 minutes, until tender. Remove from oven and cool. When cooled, scoop flesh into a large mixing bowl. Stir in the garlic, cumin seeds, parsley, mint, onion and breadcrumbs. Refrigerate for one hour.

2. Wet your hands and mold mixture into a burger shape. Add olive oil to a frying pan on medium heat. Burger will need to be cooked 6–7 minutes on each side, until golden brown and crispy around the edges.

Garlic Potato Burgers

Servings	8-10 burgers

INGREDIENTS:
- 8 oz potatoes, grated
- 3 garlic cloves, minced
- 1 teaspoon dried thyme
- 1 teaspoon paprika
- 1/2 cup breadcrumbs
- 3/4 cup all purpose flour
- 2 tablespoons olive oil
- 2 tablespoons flax seeds, ground
- 4 tablespoons water

DIRECTIONS:
1. Combine flax seeds and water in small mixing bowl and let soak.
2. Put remaining ingredient list in large mixing bowl and mix well.
3. Wet your hands and mold mixture into a burger shape. Add olive oil to a frying pan on medium heat. Burger will need to be cooked 6-7 minutes on each side, until golden brown and crispy around the edges.

Fried Burgers

Eggplant and Cauliflower Fried Burgers

Servings	6-8 burgers

INGREDIENTS:
- 1 eggplant
- 1 head cauliflower, cut into florets
- 1/2 cup rolled oats
- 2 tablespoons cornmeal
- 1 teaspoon dried basil
- 1 teaspoon dried oregano
- Salt, pepper (to taste)
- 1/4 cup flour

DIRECTIONS:

1. Preheat oven to 450 degrees. Prepare eggplant by cutting in half, generously sprinkling with salt/pepper and placing on a baking sheet. Bake the eggplant approximately 30-40 minutes, until tender. Remove from oven and cool. When cooled, scoop flesh into a large mixing bowl. Stir in the garlic, cumin seeds, parsley, mint, onion and breadcrumbs. Refrigerate for one hour.

2. Steam cauliflower 10-15 minutes, until tender. Coarsely chop them with large knife and combine them with eggplant mixture. Finish the recipe with rolled oats, cornmeal, basil and oregano.

3. Wet your hands and mold mixture into a burger shape and coat with the flour. Add olive oil to a frying pan on medium heat. Burger will need to be cooked 6-7 minutes on each side, until golden brown.

4. Serve them on vegan burger buns with your favorite toppings.

Okra Burgers

Servings	4-6 burgers

INGREDIENTS:

- 1 pound okra, finely sliced
- 1 onion, chopped
- 1/2 cup cornmeal
- 2/3 cup all purpose flour
- 1/4 teaspoon baking powder
- 1/2 cup water
- Salt, pepper (to taste)
- 1 tablespoon flax seeds, ground
- 2 tablespoons water

DIRECTIONS:

1. Mix flax seeds with water and allow to soak.
2. In a large mixing bowl, combine okra slices, onion, cornmeal, flour, baking powder and water, then stir in the flax seeds and salt/pepper.
3. Wet your hands and mold mixture into a burger shape. Add olive oil to a frying pan on medium heat. Burger will need to be cooked 6-7 minutes on each side, until golden brown.
4. Serve with your choice of bread and toppings.

Garlic Brown Rice Burgers

Servings	8-10 burgers

INGREDIENTS:
- 2 1/2 cups cooked brown rice
- 1 small onion, finely chopped
- 1 small carrot, peeled and grated
- 3 garlic cloves, minced
- 1 teaspoon sesame seeds
- Salt, pepper (to taste)

DIRECTIONS:

1. In a large mixing bowl, combine rice, carrots, garlic and onion. If the mixture doesn't stay together well, add just a bit of water to wet. Mix in sesame seeds and salt/pepper.

2. Wet your hands and mold mixture into a burger shape. Add olive oil to a frying pan on medium heat. Cook burger for 6-7 minutes on each side, until golden brown.

3. Serve with your choice of bread and toppings.

Black Bean and Lime Burgers

Servings	10-12 burgers

INGREDIENTS:
- 2 red onions, chopped
- 1 carrot, peeled and grated
- 2 tablespoons olive oil
- 1 cup mushrooms, chopped
- 1 cup canned sweet corn, drained and rinsed
- 1 teaspoon cumin seeds
- 3 cups canned black beans, drained and rinsed
- 1 chipotle pepper, deseeded and chopped
- 1/2 cup cornmeal
- 1/2 cup breadcrumbs
- Salt, pepper (to taste)

FOR THE LIME DRESSING:
- 1/2 cup sour cream
- Zest and juice from 1/2 lime
- 1/8 teaspoon cayenne pepper
- Salt to taste

DIRECTIONS:

1. In a large frying pan, cook carrots and onions in olive oil until they start to soften. Add to the frying pan: mushrooms, corn, pepper and cumin seeds, heat for ten minutes, frequently stirring. Allow pan mixture to cool.

2. In a blender, blend beans until they are fine. In a large mixing bowl, combine frying pan mixture, beans, cornmeal, and salt/pepper.

Fried Burgers

3. Wet your hands and mold mixture into a burger shape. Coat each side of burger with breadcrumbs.
4. Add olive oil to a frying pan on medium heat. Cook burger for 6-7 minutes on each side, until crispy golden brown.
5. To make the dressing, simply mix all the ingredients in a bowl.
6. Serve with your choice of bread and toppings.

Beet and Black Bean Fried Burger

Servings	6–8 burgers

INGREDIENTS:
- 1 cup cooked brown rice
- 1 small onion, finely chopped
- 2 large beets, peeled and grated
- 3 garlic cloves, minced
- 2 teaspoons cider vinegar
- 1 1/2 cups canned black beans, drained and rinsed
- 2 tablespoons olive oil
- 2 tablespoons chopped coriander leaves
- 2 tablespoons all purpose flour

DIRECTIONS:
1. In a medium frying pan, sauté onion until translucent. Add the garlic and cook 1 more minute. Add beets and cover pan, cooking on low for 10-15 minutes, stirring occasionally. Once beets are tender, stir in vinegar and remove from heat.
2. In a large mixing bowl, mash the beans with a potato masher. Add beet mixture, coriander leaves and rice, combine well. Stir in the flour and salt/pepper.
3. Wet your hands and mold mixture into a burger shape.
4. Add olive oil to a frying pan on medium heat. Cook burger for 6-7 minutes on each side, until crispy golden brown.
5. Serve with your vegan roll and your favorite condiments.

Minty Green Pea Burgers

Servings	6-8 burgers

INGREDIENTS:
- 1 head cauliflower, trimmed and cut into florets
- 1 cup green peas, frozen
- 1 teaspoon cumin
- 1 tablespoons fresh chopped mint
- 2 tablespoons fresh chopped coriander
- 1/2 cup cooked quinoa
- 2 tablespoons whole wheat flour
- 1 tablespoon flax seeds, ground
- 2 tablespoons water
- Salt, pepper (to taste)

DIRECTIONS:
1. Combine flax seeds and water in small mixing bowl.
2. Steam cauliflower and peas 10 - 15 minutes, until tender. In a large mixing bowl, mash steamed vegetable with a fork. Add flax seeds, cumin, chopped herbs, quinoa and flour, mix well.
3. Wet your hands and mold mixture into a burger shape.
4. Add olive oil to a frying pan on medium heat. Cook burger for 6-7 minutes on each side, until crispy golden brown.
5. Serve with your vegan roll and your favorite condiments.

Spicy Cilantro Burgers

Servings	8–10 burgers

INGREDIENTS:
- 3/4 cup cooked quinoa
- 2 tablespoons olive oil
- 1 small red onion, finely chopped
- 2 garlic cloves, minced
- 2 tablespoons olive oil
- 2 cups canned pinto beans, drained
- 1 teaspoon smoked paprika
- 1/2 cup chopped cilantro
- 1/2 cup cornmeal
- Salt, pepper (to taste)
- Lettuce leaves and tomato slices (for serving)
- Vegan burger buns (for serving)

FOR THE SPICY GUACAMOLE (TOPPING FOR BURGER):
- 1 ripe avocado, peeled
- 1 teaspoon lemon juice
- 1/2 teaspoon cayenne pepper
- 1 tomato, peeled, deseeded, and diced
- 1 red onion, finely chopped
- 2 tablespoons coconut cream

DIRECTIONS:
1. Sauté onion and garlic in large frying pan for three minutes. Add beans and paprika and continue to sauté another two minutes. In a medium mixing bowl, mash the mixture with a fork.

Fried Burgers

2. In a large mixing bowl, add bean mixture, stir in the cooked quinoa, cilantro, half the cornmeal and salt/pepper.
3. Wet your hands and mold mixture into a burger shape. Coat burgers with remaining cornmeal.
4. Add olive oil to a frying pan on medium heat. Cook burger for 4 minutes on each side, until crispy golden brown. Dab with a paper towel to get rid of excess grease.
5. Serve with your vegan roll and a spoonful of guacamole topping. To make: put flesh of avocado, lemon juice together in small mixing bowl, mash with fork. Stir in remaining guacamole ingredients listed and mix well.

Wheat Germ/Pumpkin Burgers

Servings	6–8 burgers

INGREDIENTS:
- 1/4 cup olive oil
- 1 small red onion, finely chopped
- 1 red bell pepper, cored and chopped
- 3 oz sweet corn, fresh or frozen
- 2 garlic cloves, minced
- 1 teaspoon chili powder
- 1 teaspoon cumin powder
- 1 cup canned pumpkin puree
- 1/2 cup wheat germ
- 1/3 cup breadcrumbs
- 2 tablespoons all purpose flour
- 2 tablespoons chopped coriander

DIRECTIONS:
1. Sauté onion in large frying pan until translucent. Add red bell pepper, sweet corn, chili powder, cumin and garlic ingredients, cook for 5 minutes, covered with a lid. Remove from heat and cool before transferring to a large mixing bowl.
2. Add to this large mixing bowl, pumpkin puree, breadcrumbs, wheat germ, flour, coriander and salt/pepper. Mix well to combine.
3. Wet your hands and mold spoonfuls of the mixture into a burger shape.

Fried Burgers

4. Add olive oil to a frying pan on medium heat. Cook burger for 4-5 minutes on each side, until crispy golden brown around the edges.
5. Serve with your vegan roll and top with shredded cabbage.

Almond Lentil Burgers

Servings	6–8 burgers

INGREDIENTS:
- 1 cup green lentils
- 5 cups water
- 3 tablespoons extra virgin olive oil
- 1 large carrot, peeled and finely chopped
- 1 shallot, chopped
- 2 garlic cloves, minced
- 1 celery stick, finely chopped
- 1/4 cup sliced almonds
- 1 tablespoon flax seeds, ground
- 2 tablespoons water
- Salt, pepper (to taste)

DIRECTIONS:
1. Put the water into a medium saucepan and bring to a boil. Add lentils and cook for 20 minutes, lentils will be tender. Allow lentils to cool.
2. Mix flax seed with 2 tablespoons of water and let set while the lentils are cooling.
3. Cook shallot with three tablespoons of olive oil in a large frying pan until tender. Add garlic, sauté two minutes using low heat. Add carrot and celery, cook until tender, approximately eight minutes, stirring frequently.
4. Make a paste with half of the cooled lentils in a food processor. Put pasted in a large mixing bowl. Add the remaining lentils, flax seeds, shallot mixture and the sliced almonds, mix well.

Fried Burgers

5. Wet your hands and mold mixture into a burger shape.
6. Add olive oil to a frying pan on medium heat. Cook burger for 4–5 minutes on each side, until crispy golden brown.
7. Serve with your vegan roll and your favorite condiments.

Tofu Tomato Burgers

Servings	8-10 burgers

INGREDIENTS:

- 1/4 cup sun-dried tomatoes, drained
- 1 cup water
- 1/2 cup millet, rinsed
- 1 1/2 cup vegetable stock
- 1/4 cup extra virgin olive oil
- 1 small onion, chopped
- 2 garlic cloves, minced
- 4 cups baby spinach leaves
- 2 tablespoons chopped fresh basil
- 1/2 cup breadcrumbs
- 1/2 cup firm tofu, crumbled
- Salt, pepper (to taste)

DIRECTIONS:

1. Put tomatoes and water in a medium saucepan. Bring to a boil for one minute, remove from heat and let soak for one hour. Drain water and finely chop tomatoes.

2. Pour vegetable stock into empty saucepan and bring to a boil. Add millet and simmer for 25 minutes, until water has been absorbed. Let cool and add to a large mixing bowl.

3. Sauté onion, garlic, and two tablespoons of olive oil for 4-5 minutes on low heat until translucent. Add spinach, cook for one minute. Remove from heat and add to millet mixing bowl.

Fried Burgers

4. When completely cold, add millet mixture to a food process and pulse until smooth. Place back into the large mixing bowl. Stir in crumbled tofu, basil, breadcrumbs, tomatoes and salt/pepper.
5. Wet your hands and mold mixture into a burger shape.
6. Add olive oil to a frying pan on medium heat. Cook burger for 4-5 minutes on each side, until crispy golden brown around the edges of burger.
7. Serve with your vegan roll and your favorite condiments.

Mushroom Pecan Burgers

Servings	6-8 burgers

INGREDIENTS:
- 1 pound cremini mushrooms
- 2 tablespoons packed parsley leaves
- 2 tablespoons olive oil
- 1 onion, chopped
- 2 garlic cloves, minced
- 1 cup breadcrumbs
- 3 oz pecans
- 2 teaspoons soy sauce
- 3 tablespoon tahini sauce
- 1 teaspoon dried oregano
- Salt, pepper (to taste)

DIRECTIONS:
1. Grind mushrooms and pecans in a food processor. Put ground mixture into large mixing bowl.
2. Sauté the onion and garlic in a large frying pan until onion is translucent. Put onion mixture, mushrooms and breadcrumbs in large mixing bowl with mushroom mixture. Add soy sauce, tahini paste, chopped parsley and dried oregano, combine.
3. Wet your hands and mold mixture into a burger shape.
4. Add olive oil to a frying pan on medium heat. Cook burger for 6-7 minutes on each side, until crispy golden brown around the edges of burger.

Fried Burgers

Soybean Tofu Burgers

Servings	8–10 burgers

INGREDIENTS:
- 3 cups canned soybeans, drained
- 6 oz firm tofu
- 1 onion, chopped
- 1 celery stalk, chopped
- 1 1/2 cup rolled oats
- 1/2 teaspoon nutritional yeast
- 2 tablespoons flax seeds, ground
- 6 tablespoons water
- 2 tablespoons wheat gluten
- 1 teaspoon soy sauce
- 1 tablespoon olive oil
- Salt, pepper (to taste)

DIRECTIONS:
1. Combine flax seeds and water and allow to set for ten minutes.
2. In a food processor, pulse together soybeans, tofu, olive oil and yeast until smooth in texture. Put mixture in large mixing bowl. Add celery, onion, flax seeds, rolled oats, yeast, gluten and soy sauce, mix well.
3. Wet your hands and mold mixture into a burger shape.
4. Add olive oil to a frying pan on medium heat. Cook burger for 4-5 minutes on each side, until crispy golden brown around the edges of burger.
5. Serve with your vegan roll and your favorite condiments.

Paprika Pepper Burgers

Servings	8-10 burgers

INGREDIENTS:
- 4 cups cooked lentils
- 1 red onion, chopped
- 2 garlic cloves, minced
- 2 bell peppers, roasted and peeled
- 2 tablespoons fresh parsley, chopped
- 1/2 cup breadcrumbs
- 1 teaspoon smoked paprika
- 1 teaspoon cumin
- 1 teaspoon nutritional yeast
- 2 tablespoons flax seeds, ground
- 6 tablespoons water
- Salt, pepper (to taste)

DIRECTIONS:
1. Combine flax seeds and water and allow to set for ten minutes.
2. In food processor pulse to combine 2 cups of lentils, bell peppers and all spices. In a large mixing bowl, add spice mixture, remaining lentils, flax seed mixture, nutritional yeast, garlic, onion, parsley and breadcrumbs. Mix well.
3. Wet your hands and mold mixture into a burger shape.
4. Add olive oil to a frying pan on medium heat. Cook burger for 4-5 minutes on each side, until crispy golden brown around the edges of burger.
5. Serve with your vegan roll and your favorite condiments.

Fried Burgers

Carrot Zucchini Burgers

Servings	4-6 burgers

INGREDIENTS:
- 1 zucchini, grated
- 1 carrot, peeled and grated
- 3 tablespoons flour
- Salt, pepper (to taste)

DIRECTIONS:
1. Combine all ingredients in a large mixing bowl.
2. Wet your hands and mold mixture into a burger shape.
3. Add olive oil to a frying pan on medium heat. Cook burger for 6-7 minutes on each side, until crispy golden brown around the edges of burger.
4. Serve with your vegan roll and your favorite condiments.

Sweet Potato Burgers with Basil and Onion

Servings	2-4 burgers

INGREDIENTS:
- 2 sweet potatoes, washed
- 4 tablespoons fresh chopped basil
- 2 tablespoons rolled oats
- 2 tablespoons whole wheat flour
- 1 green onion, chopped
- Salt, pepper (to taste)

DIRECTIONS:
1. Preheat oven to 400 degrees. Wrap the two sweet potatoes with tin foil and bake for approximately 40 minutes. In a large mixing bowl, place the flesh of the potatoes, and mash with a fork. Add basil, green onion, oats and flour, and combine.
2. Wet your hands and mold a large spoonful of the mixture into a burger shape.
3. Add olive oil to a frying pan on medium heat. Cook burger for 4-5 minutes on each side, until crispy golden brown around the edges of burger.
4. Serve with your vegan roll, favorite toppings and condiments.

Fried Burgers

Sun-dried Tomatoes and Black Bean Burgers

Servings	8–10 burgers

INGREDIENTS:
- 4 oz sun-dried tomatoes
- 2 cups warm water
- 3 cups canned black beans, rinsed/drained
- 1 teaspoon cumin
- 1/2 teaspoon dried oregano
- 2 tablespoons fresh chopped basil
- 1 cup rolled oats
- 1 cup cooked brown rice
- Salt, pepper (to taste)

DIRECTIONS:
1. In a large mixing bowl, combine tomatoes and water, let soak for thirty minutes, drain, and finely chop.
2. In a food processor, pulse the beans until they are smooth. Put beans in a large mixing bowl, stir in the chopped tomatoes, cumin, oregano, basil, oats, brown rice, and salt/pepper.
3. Wet your hands and mold a large spoonful of the mixture into a burger shape.
4. Add olive oil to a frying pan on medium heat. Cook burger for 4–5 minutes on each side, until crispy golden brown around the edges of burger.
5. Serve with your vegan roll, favorite toppings and condiments.

Tofu Burgers with Cayenne Pepper

Servings	4-6 burgers

INGREDIENTS:
- 3 cups frozen spinach, thawed and drained
- 2 tablespoons flax seeds, ground
- 4 tablespoons water
- 1 onion, finely chopped
- 4 oz tofu, crumbled
- 1/2 cup breadcrumbs
- 2 garlic cloves, minced
- 1/4 teaspoon cayenne pepper
- Salt (to taste)

DIRECTIONS:
1. Combine flax seeds and water and allow to set for ten minutes.
2. Remove all water from spinach by squeezing it. In large mixing bowl, stir spinach, onion, crumbled tofu, breadcrumbs, garlic, pepper flax seeds, and salt/pepper together.
3. Wet your hands and mold a large spoonful of the mixture into a burger shape.
4. Add olive oil to a frying pan on medium heat. Cook burger for 4-5 minutes on each side, until crispy golden brown around the edges of burger.

Baked Burgers

Parsley Sweet Potato Burgers

Servings	4–6 burgers

INGREDIENTS:
- 2 sweet potatoes, peeled and cubed
- 1 cup rolled oats
- 3 green onions, finely chopped
- 1/2 cup chopped parsley
- Salt, pepper (to taste)

DIRECTIONS:
1. Preheat oven to 400 degrees. Steam the sweet potatoes approximately fifteen minutes, until tender. Mash them with a fork in a large mixing bowl. Combine potatoes with the rest of the ingredients list.
2. Line a 13×9 pan with parchment paper and evenly space the burgers apart. Cook approx 30–40 minutes, until golden brown.
3. Serve them with your choice of bun, toppings, and condiments.

Red Potato Quinoa Burgers

Servings	6-8 burgers

INGREDIENTS:

- 2 teaspoons flax seeds, ground
- 4 tablespoons water
- 1 1/2 cup canned white beans, drained
- 1 1/2 cups cooked quinoa
- 2 red potatoes, cubed, boiled, and mashed
- 1 teaspoon nutritional yeast
- 1 small red onion, finely chopped
- 2 tablespoons all purpose flour
- 2 garlic cloves
- 1/2 cup packed fresh basil, chopped
- Salt, pepper (to taste)

DIRECTIONS:

1. Preheat oven to 375 degrees. Combine flax seeds and water and allow to set for ten minutes.
2. In a food processor, pulse beans until a paste forms. In a large mixing bowl, combine paste with entire ingredient list.
3. Form mixture into a burger shape using wet hands. Line a 13x9 baking pan with parchment paper and evenly distribute burgers in the pan. Cook approximately 40 minutes, until burgers are golden brown.

Portobello Burgers Marmalade

Servings	4 burgers

INGREDIENTS:
- 4 Portobello mushrooms
- 1 small zucchini, diced
- 1 onion, finely chopped
- 1 tomato, peeled, deseeded, and diced
- 2 tablespoons packed basil leaves, chopped
- Salt, pepper (to taste)

FOR THE ONION MARMALADE:
- 3 red onions, sliced
- 1 cup sugar
- 1/2 cup vinegar
- 1 cinnamon stick

DIRECTIONS:

1. Preheat oven to 375 degrees. Combine zucchini, onion, tomato and basil in a large mixing bowl. In a 13×9 baking pan, evenly distribute the mushrooms and spoon mixture from mixing bowl into each. Bake approximately 25 minutes.

2. To make the marmalade: In a medium saucepan, cook onion, sugar, vinegar and cinnamon stick on medium heat. Bring to a boil for one minute and then simmer until almost all of the liquid has evaporated.

3. Serve mushrooms warm with warm marmalade over them.

Parsley Bulgur Burgers

Servings	6-8 burgers

INGREDIENTS:
- 4 cups water
- 1 1/4 cup uncooked bulgur
- 2 cups chopped parsley leaves
- 1 cucumber, diced
- 1 tomato, peeled, deseeded, and diced
- 2 tablespoons chopped mint leaves
- 4 tablespoons olive oil
- 3 garlic cloves, minced
- Juice from 1/2 lemon
- 2 tablespoons cornstarch
- 1 cup whole wheat flour

DIRECTIONS:
1. Preheat oven to 375 degrees. Bring water to a boil in a large saucepan, add bulgur. Boil for one minute, and reduce heat to simmer for fifteen minutes, or until all water has evaporated. Allow bulgur to cool.
2. In a large mixing bowl, add cooled bulgur, parsley, mint, cucumber, tomato, garlic, lemon juice, olive oil and salt/pepper. Combine and stir in flour and cornstarch.
3. Line a 13x9 baking pan with parchment paper. Wet hands and form mixture into a burger shape and evenly distribute in pan. Bake for 40 minutes, until browned and crusty around the edges.

Brown Rice Carrot Burgers

Servings	6–8 burgers

INGREDIENTS:
- 10 oz fresh spinach, chopped
- 2 tablespoons olive oil
- 1 leek, finely chopped
- 1 carrot, peeled and grated
- 2 garlic cloves, minced
- 1 teaspoon dried oregano
- 1/4 cup cooked brown rice
- 1 package firm tofu, crumbled
- 2 tablespoons fresh chopped dill
- Salt/pepper (to taste)

DIRECTIONS:

1. Preheat oven to 350 degrees. Sauté leeks, carrot, garlic and dried oregano in a large frying pan, until carrots are tender. Add spinach and cook for one minute. Allow to cool.

2. In a food processor, puree tofu. Put half of the spinach mixture and pulse a few more times to combine. Put food processor ingredients into a large mixing bowl and stir in the rest of the spinach mixture from the frying pan. Add brown rice, dill, and salt/pepper, combine.

3. Line a 13×9 baking pan with parchment paper. Wet hands and form mixture into a burger shape and evenly distribute in pan. Bake for 40 minutes, until browned and crusty around the edges.

Tofu Burgers with Corn

Servings	8–10 burgers

Ingredients:
- 1 cup frozen sweet corn
- 1/2 cup walnuts
- 1 package firm tofu, crumbled
- 2 garlic cloves
- 1 carrot, peeled and grated
- 1/2 cup cornmeal
- 1/2 cup flour
- 1 tablespoon tahini paste
- 2 tablespoons chopped coriander
- 1 teaspoon cumin powder
- salt, pepper (to taste)

Directions:
1. Preheat oven to 350 degrees. In a food processor, combine half the corn, walnuts, and coriander. Put in a large mixing bowl. Add remainder of ingredients list and combine.

2. Line a 13×9 baking pan with parchment paper. Wet hands and form mixture into a burger shape and evenly distribute in pan. Bake for 40 minutes, until browned and crusty around the edges.

Garlic Tofu Burger

Servings	8-10 burgers

INGREDIENTS:
- 15 oz firm tofu, drained well
- 1 tablespoon dried parsley
- 2 tablespoons dried basil
- 1 tablespoons fresh chopped thyme
- 1 teaspoon dried rosemary
- 1 cup cooked brown rice
- 2 garlic cloves, minced
- 2 tablespoons flax seeds, ground
- 4 tablespoons water
- 1/2 cup seeds mix (sunflower, pumpkin)
- Salt, pepper (to taste)

DIRECTIONS:
1. Preheat oven to 350 degrees. Combine flax seed and water and let stand for ten minutes.
2. In a large mixing bowl, add crumbled tofu, all herbs listed and mix well. Add remaining ingredients from the list and mix well.
3. Line a 13×9 baking pan with parchment paper. Wet hands and form mixture into a burger shape and evenly distribute in pan, drizzle top with olive oil. Bake for 25 minutes, until browned and crusty around the edges.

Black-eye Pea Burgers

Servings	6–8 burgers

INGREDIENTS:

- 5 oz cremini mushrooms, thinly sliced
- 1 red onion, chopped
- 2 garlic cloves, minced
- 2 tablespoons olive oil
- 2 cups canned black-eyed peas
- 2 tablespoons chopped parsley
- 1 teaspoon soy sauce
- 1/2 teaspoon chili flakes
- Salt, pepper (to paste)

DIRECTIONS:

1. Preheat oven to 400 degrees. Sauté onion in large frying pan with olive oil. When onion is translucent, add mushrooms and garlic, cook additional ten minutes. Allow to cool.

2. Mash peas by blending them in a blender. In a large mixing bowl, combine mushroom mixture and peas. Combine with soy sauce and chili flakes.

3. Line a 13×9 baking pan with parchment paper. Wet hands and form mixture into a burger shape and evenly distribute in pan. Bake for 25–30 minutes, until browned and crusty around the edges.

Chickpea Artichoke Burgers

Servings	6-8 BURGERS

INGREDIENTS:
- 7 oz artichoke hearts, drained and chopped
- 2 garlic cloves, minced
- 2 tablespoons fresh chopped parsley
- 1 cup canned chickpeas, drained
- 1 cup canned kidney beans, drained
- 2 tablespoons tahini paste
- 1 carrot, peeled and grated
- 3 tablespoons flax seeds
- 1/2 cup rolled oats
- Salt, pepper (to taste)

DIRECTIONS:

1. Preheat oven to 400 degrees. Put all ingredients in food processor and pulse until well blended, but still chunky.

2. Line a 13×9 baking pan with parchment paper. Wet hands and form mixture into a burger shape and evenly distribute in pan. Bake for 25-30 minutes, until browned and crusty around the edges.

Sunflower Cumin Burgers

Servings	4-6 burgers

INGREDIENTS:
- 4 carrot, peeled and grated
- 1 small onion, finely chopped
- 2 garlic cloves, minced
- 1 tablespoon olive oil
- 1 teaspoon cumin
- 1/2 cup walnuts, chopped
- 2 tablespoons sunflower seeds
- 1 cup canned chickpeas
- 1 cup cooked quinoa
- 2 tablespoons chopped parsley
- Salt, pepper (to taste)
- 1/4 cup whole wheat flour

DIRECTIONS:

1. Sauté onion and garlic with olive oil in a medium frying pan for 2-3 minutes. Add cumin and cook one additional minute.
1. In a food processor, pulse the chickpeas until smooth paste forms. Put paste in a large mixing bowl and add remainder of ingredient list, minus the whole wheat flour.
1. Line a 13×9 baking pan with parchment paper. Wet hands and form mixture into a burger shape, coating each side with whole wheat flour, and evenly distribute burgers in pan. Preheat oven to 325 degrees, chill burgers for 30 minutes. Remove from refrigerator and bake for approximately 30 minutes, until browned and crusty around the edges.

Baked Burgers

Millet Vegetable Burgers

Servings	6–8 burgers

INGREDIENTS:
- 1 1/4 cup millet
- 3 1/2 cups water or vegetable broth
- 1 carrot, peeled and grated
- 1 small onion, chopped
- 2 garlic cloves, minced
- 2 tablespoons olive oil
- 1/4 cup breadcrumbs
- 1 teaspoon Italian seasoning
- 1/4 cup sesame seeds
- Salt, pepper (to taste)

DIRECTIONS:

1. Preheat oven to 350 degrees. Roast millet for 3-4 minutes to enhance flavor. Bring broth to a boil in a large saucepan. Add millet and reduce heat to low, cooking until all broth has been absorbed. Put in a large mixing bowl.

2. 2. Sauté the onion and garlic with olive oil for 2 minutes, add to millet mixture. Combine all other ingredients, except for the sesame seeds.

3. Line a 13×9 baking pan with parchment paper. Wet hands and form mixture into a burger shape, evenly coat each side of burger with sesame seeds, and evenly distribute in pan. Bake for 40 minutes, until browned and crusty around the edges.

Lentil Peanut Butter Burgers

Servings	8-10 burgers

INGREDIENTS:
- 1 1/2 cup cooked brown rice
- 1 1/2 cup canned brown lentils
- 1 carrot, peeled and grated
- 1 cup whole wheat breadcrumbs
- 1/2 cup peanut butter
- 1 teaspoon soy sauce
- 1 teaspoon dried oregano
- 2 tablespoons chopped parsley
- 1 teaspoon smoked paprika
- Salt, pepper (to taste)

DIRECTIONS:
1. Preheat oven to 400 degrees. In a large mixing bowl, combine all ingredients listed.
2. Line a 13×9 baking pan with parchment paper. Wet hands and form mixture into a burger shape, and evenly distribute in pan. Bake for 30 minutes, until browned and crusty around the edges.

Lemon Chickpea Burgers

Servings	6–8 burgers

INGREDIENTS:
- 2 cups canned chickpeas, drained
- 1 small onion, chopped
- 1/3 cup chopped coriander
- 1 teaspoon cumin
- 1 teaspoon lemon juice
- 2 tablespoons flour
- 2 tablespoons olive oil
- Salt, pepper (to taste)

DIRECTIONS:
1. Preheat oven to 400 degrees. Pulse all ingredients in a food processor until well combined, but still chunky.
2. Line a 13×9 baking pan with parchment paper. Wet hands and form mixture into a burger shape, and evenly distribute in pan. Bake for 30–40 minutes, until browned and crusty around the edges.

Oat and Pine Nut Burgers

Servings	8-10 burgers

INGREDIENTS:
- 2 cups canned lentils, drained
- 1 green onion, chopped
- 1 garlic clove, minced
- 1/2 cup rolled oats
- 1 tablespoon flour
- 1/8 teaspoon cayenne pepper
- 1 cup packed basil leaves
- 1/2 cup pine nuts
- 4 tablespoons olive oil
- 1 teaspoon lemon juice
- Salt, pepper (to taste)

DIRECTIONS:
1. Preheat oven to 400 degrees. In a food processor, pulse half of the lentils, onion and garlic until a paste forms. Put the paste in a large mixing bowl. Add remaining lentils, oats, flour and salt/pepper and combine.
2. Line a 13×9 baking pan with parchment paper. Wet hands and form mixture into a burger shape, and evenly distribute in pan. Bake for 30-40 minutes, until browned and crusty around the edges.
3. To make the Pesto: In a food processor, pulse together the basil leaves, pine nuts and lemon juice, gradually adding the olive oil. Pulse until smooth.
4. Serve the burgers on vegan bun with a spoonful of pesto.

Raisin Walnut Burgers

Servings	4-6 burgers

INGREDIENTS:
- 1 small onion, chopped
- 2 tablespoons olive oil
- 2/3 cup walnuts
- 1/2 cup raisins
- 1 beetroot, peeled and grated
- 1 teaspoon smoked paprika
- 1/2 cup canned lentils, drained
- 1 tablespoon flax seeds, ground
- 3 tablespoons water
- 1 2/3 cups cooked brown rice
- Salt, pepper (to taste)

DIRECTIONS:

1. Preheat oven to 400 degrees. Combine flax seeds and water, allow to soak ten minutes. Sauté onion until translucent in a large frying pan, about five minutes. Add garlic, walnuts, raisins, beetroots and paprika to frying pan, cook ten minutes. In a food processor, combine frying pan ingredients until well blended and chunky.

2. Transfer food processor blend to a large mixing bowl and combine with remaining ingredients on the list. Line a 13×9 baking pan with parchment paper. Wet hands and form mixture into a burger shape, and evenly distribute in pan. Bake for 30-40 minutes, until browned and crusty around the edges.

3. Serve on vegan burger with your favorite toppings.

Pumpkin Oat Burgers

Servings	6-8 burgers

INGREDIENTS:
- 2/3 cup pumpkin puree, canned
- 2 garlic cloves
- 1 cup cooked brown rice
- 2 cups black beans
- 1 teaspoon cumin
- 1/2 teaspoon chili powder
- 2 tablespoons flax seeds, ground
- 1/2 cup rolled oats
- 1/4 cup breadcrumbs
- 2 tablespoons pumpkin seeds
- Salt, pepper (to taste)

DIRECTIONS:

1. Preheat oven to 375 degrees. Pulse beans in a food processor until smooth. In a large mixing bowl, add the beans and remaining ingredient list and combine.

2. Line a 13x9 baking pan with parchment paper. Wet hands and form mixture into a burger shape, and evenly distribute in pan. Bake for 30-40 minutes, until browned and crusty around the edges.

3. Serve on vegan buns with your favorite toppings.

Garlic Oatmeal Burgers

Servings	4–6 burgers

INGREDIENTS:

- 2 cups canned white beans, drained
- 2 garlic cloves
- 1 onion, finely chopped
- 2 tablespoons olive oil
- 2 cups chopped kale
- 1 teaspoon lemon juice
- 1 cup rolled oats
- Salt, pepper (to taste)

DIRECTIONS:

1. Preheat oven to 400 degrees. Sauté onion in large frying pan until translucent. Add garlic and kale to pan and cook until soft. Allow to cool.

2. Pulse beans in food processor until smooth. In a large mixing bowl, combine kale mixture, beans, and remaining ingredients. Line a 13×9 baking pan with parchment paper. Wet hands and form mixture into a burger shape, and evenly distribute in pan. Bake for 30–40 minutes, until browned and crusty around the edges.

3. Serve with bread of choice, toppings, and condiments.

Sunflower Burgers with Garlic Sauce

Servings	4-6 burgers

INGREDIENTS:
- 2 cups canned green lentils, drained and rinsed
- 2 tablespoons olive oil
- 1 green onion, chopped
- 1 garlic clove, chopped
- 1 carrot, peeled and grated
- 1/2 cup sunflower seeds
- 1/2 cup breadcrumbs
- 2 tablespoons rolled oats
- Salt, pepper (to taste)

FOR THE SAUCE:
- 1/2 cup vegan yogurt
- 1/2 teaspoon ginger
- 2 garlic cloves

DIRECTIONS:
1. In a food processor, pulse lentils until smooth. In a large mixing bowl, combine lentils with rest of ingredient list for the burger.
2. Line a 13x9 baking pan with parchment paper. Wet hands and form mixture into a burger shape, and evenly distribute in pan. Refrigerate burgers for 30 minutes.
3. Preheat oven to 400 degrees. Bake for 30-40 minutes, until browned and crusty around the edges.
4. To make the sauce: mix all ingredients in a small mixing bowl.

Herbed Tofu Burgers

Servings	4–6 burgers

INGREDIENTS:
- 1/2 cup chopped green onions
- 1 pound herbed firm tofu
- 1/2 cup breadcrumbs
- 1/2 cup black sesame seeds
- 1 teaspoon soy sauce
- 1 teaspoon fresh grated ginger
- 3 oz sushi wrapping
- Salt, pepper (to taste)

DIRECTIONS:

1. Bring two cups of water to a boil in a large saucepan. Remove saucepan from burner and put sushi wrap in pan, stir well. Allow to soak ten minutes and drain well. Preheat oven to 375 degrees.

2. In a food processor, put half of the tofu, green onion and sushi wrap, pulse until well blended. Add mixture to a large mixing bowl, combine with breadcrumbs, soy sauce, fresh ginger, and salt/pepper.

3. Line a 13×9 baking pan with parchment paper. Wet hands and form mixture into a burger shape, coat both sides of each burger with sesame seeds, and evenly distribute in pan. Bake for 40 minutes, until browned and crusty around the edges.

Roasted Eggplant Burgers

Servings	4-6 burgers

INGREDIENTS:

- 2 red bell peppers, roasted and peeled
- 1 eggplant
- 1 teaspoon cumin
- 1 tablespoon olive oil
- 1/2 cup rolled oats
- 2/3 cup whole wheat breadcrumbs
- 2 tablespoons chopped parsley
- 2 tablespoons chopped coriander
- Salt, pepper (to taste)

DIRECTIONS:

1. Preheat oven to 350 degrees. Cut the eggplant in half and put it in a baking pan, drizzle with olive oil and sprinkle with cumin. Bake for 30 minutes, until tender, and scoop flesh into a large mixing bowl.

2. Dice the peppers and put into the eggplant bowl. Add remaining ingredients to bowl and mix well..

3. Line a 13×9 baking pan with parchment paper. Wet hands and form mixture into a burger shape, and evenly distribute in pan. Bake for 30-40 minutes, until browned and crusty around the edges.

Baked Burgers

Beetroot Burgers and Barley Salad

Servings	6–8 burgers

INGREDIENTS:

For burgers:
- 2 beetroots, peeled and grated
- 1 cup rolled oats
- 1 cup canned chickpeas, drained
- 1 tablespoon fresh chopped dill
- 1 tablespoon fresh chopped parsley
- 1 teaspoon fresh chopped thyme
- 2 green onions, finely chopped
- Salt, pepper (to taste)

For salad:
- 1 cup barley
- 1 celery stalk, sliced
- 1 cup chopped parsley
- 2 teaspoons balsamic vinegar
- 1 tablespoon olive oil

DIRECTIONS:

To make the burgers:

1. Preheat oven to 375 degrees. In a food processor, pulse the chickpeas until a paste forms. Put in a large mixing bowl with remaining ingredient list for burger and mix well.

2. Line a 13×9 baking pan with parchment paper. Wet hands and form mixture into a burger shape, and evenly distribute in pan. Bake for 30 minutes, until browned and crusty around the edges.

To make the salad:

1. In a large serving bowl, combine the barley, parsley, and celery. Drizzle olive oil and vinegar over the salad.

Baked Burgers

Potato Bean Burgers

Servings	6-8 burgers

INGREDIENTS:
- 1 pound potatoes, washed
- 1 cup canned white beans
- 2 tablespoons fresh chopped dill
- 1/2 teaspoon fresh chopped thyme
- 1/2 cup rolled oats
- 1 carrot, peeled and grated
- Salt, pepper (to taste)

DIRECTIONS:
1. Preheat oven to 375 degrees. Wrap potatoes in tin foil and bake approximately 40 minutes, until tender. After potatoes are tender, remove from oven, scoop the flesh into a large mixing bowl, combine with dill, thyme, rolled oats, carrot and salt/pepper.
2. In a separate mixing bowl, mash the beans with a potato masher and then combine with potato mixture bowl.
3. Line a 13×9 baking pan with parchment paper. Wet hands and form mixture into a burger shape, and evenly distribute in pan. Bake for 20-30 minutes, until golden brown.
4. To make aioli: Mix 1/2 cup vegan yogurt, three minced garlic cloves and salt/pepper to taste.
5. Serve the burgers on buns with a spoonful of aioli.

Italian Courgette Burgers

Servings	6–8 burgers

INGREDIENTS:
- 2 courgettes, grated
- 2 garlic cloves, minced
- 1 tablespoon flax seeds, ground
- 2/3 cup breadcrumbs
- 1 teaspoon Italian seasoning
- 3 tablespoons all purpose flour
- Salt, pepper (to taste)
- 2 tablespoons olive oil

DIRECTIONS:
1. Preheat oven to 375 degrees. Combine flax seeds and two tablespoons of water and let soak for ten minutes.
2. In a large mixing bowl, combine all ingredients remaining and the flax seed mixture, except for the olive oil.
3. Line a 13×9 baking pan with parchment paper. Wet hands and form mixture into a burger shape, and evenly distribute in pan. Drizzle with olive oil, bake for 20–30 minutes, until browned and crusty around the edges.

Cayenne Celery Burgers

Servings	6–8 burgers

INGREDIENTS:
- 1 onion, chopped
- 1 celery stalk, chopped
- 2 tablespoons olive oil
- 3 cups canned chickpeas, drained and rinsed
- 1 teaspoon fresh chopped thyme
- 1 teaspoon cayenne pepper
- 3 tablespoons chopped parsley
- 2 tablespoons flour
- Salt, pepper (to taste)

DIRECTIONS:
1. Preheat oven to 350 degrees. In a large frying pan, sauté onion, celery, and olive oil. In a food processor, pulse onion mixture and chickpeas until well blended, but still chunky. In a large mixing bowl, combine chickpea blend with thyme, cayenne pepper, parsley, flour and salt/pepper.

2. Line a 13×9 baking pan with parchment paper. Wet hands and form mixture into a burger shape, and evenly distribute in pan. Bake for 30 minutes, until golden brown.

Lentil Broccoli Burgers

Servings	6-8 burgers

INGREDIENTS:
- 1 cup canned beans, drained
- 1/2 cup cooked peas
- 1 tomato, peeled, deseeded, and finely diced
- 1 head broccoli, shredded
- 1/2 cup pumpkin puree
- 1 tablespoon flour
- Salt, pepper (to taste)

DIRECTIONS:

1. Preheat oven to 350 degrees. In a large mixing bowl, mash beans and peas with a potato masher. Combine with the tomato, shredded broccoli, pumpkin purée and flour.

2. Line a 13×9 baking pan with parchment paper. Wet hands and form mixture into a burger shape, and evenly distribute in pan. Bake for 30-40 minutes, until browned and crusty around the edges.

Almond/Peanut Butter Burger

Servings	6-8 burgers

INGREDIENTS:

- 10 oz plain tempeh
- 1 cup flour
- 3 tablespoons almond butter
- 1 tablespoon maple syrup
- 3 tablespoons peanut butter
- 1/2 teaspoon smoked paprika
- Salt, pepper (to taste)

DIRECTIONS:

1. Preheat oven to 375 degrees. Crumble tempeh in a large mixing bowl. Combine with flour, butter, maple syrup, peanut butter, paprika, and salt/pepper.

2. Line a 13×9 baking pan with parchment paper. Wet hands and form mixture into a burger shape, and evenly distribute in pan. Bake for 20-30 minutes, until golden brown.

Coriander Mint Burgers

Servings	8-10 burgers

INGREDIENTS:
- 1 cup uncooked bulgur
- 3 cups water or vegetable broth
- 3 cups fresh chopped parsley
- 1 cup fresh chopped coriander
- 1/4 cup fresh chopped mint
- 3 tomatoes, peeled, deseeded, and diced
- 4 garlic cloves, minced
- 1 cucumber, diced
- juice from 1/2 lemon
- 1 cup whole wheat flour
- 1/4 cup cornstarch
- 2 tablespoons olive oil.
- Salt, pepper (to taste)

DIRECTIONS:

1. Bring water to a boil in a large saucepan. Add bulgur, boil for one minute, and turn heat down to low, stirring occasionally, until all liquid has been absorbed. Put bulgur in a large mixing bowl, combine with all other ingredients listed in recipe.

2. Line a 13×9 baking pan with parchment paper. Wet hands and form mixture into a burger shape, and evenly distribute in pan. Bake for 20 minutes, until golden brown.

Baked Burgers

Broccoli Cauliflower Burgers

Servings	8-10 burgers

INGREDIENTS:
- 1/2 head cauliflower, cut into florets
- 1/2 head broccoli, cut into florets
- 1 carrot, peeled and grated
- 1/2 teaspoon dried oregano
- 1 teaspoon dried basil
- 1/2 cup rolled oats
- 1/2 cup all purpose flour
- 2 tablespoons olive oil
- 1/2 teaspoon hot sauce
- Salt, pepper
- 2 tablespoons flax seeds
- 4 tablespoons water

DIRECTIONS:
1. Preheat oven to 370 degrees. Soak flax seeds and water in a small mixing bowl for ten minutes.
2. Steam broccoli and cauliflower approximately 20 minutes, until tender. Mash them in a large mixing bowl. Combine with grated carrot, dried herbs, rolled oats, flour, oil, hot sauce, flax seeds and salt/pepper.
3. Line a 13×9 baking pan with parchment paper. Wet hands and form mixture into a burger shape, and evenly distribute in pan. Bake for 30-40 minutes, until golden brown.
4. Serve with vegan buns and shredded cabbage.

Quinoa Carrot Burgers

Servings	6–8 burgers

INGREDIENTS:
- 8 oz fava beans, frozen
- 1 cup cooked quinoa
- 1 carrot, grated
- 1/2 cup rolled oats
- 2 green onions, finely chopped
- 1 garlic clove, minced
- 2 tablespoons flour
- Salt, pepper (to taste)

DIRECTIONS:

1. Preheat oven to 375 degrees. Put three cups of water in a large saucepan and bring to a boil. Cook fava beans in water for twenty minutes. Drain them and pulse in a food processor until smooth.

2. In a large mixing bowl, combine with cooked quinoa, flour, onions, garlic, rolled oats and salt/pepper.

3. Line a 13×9 baking pan with parchment paper. Wet hands and form mixture into a burger shape, and evenly distribute in pan. Bake for 30-40 minutes, until golden brown.

Cauliflower Leek Burgers

Servings	4-6 burgers

INGREDIENTS:
- 1 cauliflower head, trimmed and cut into florets
- 2 leeks, finely sliced
- 1 carrot, peeled and grated
- 2 tablespoons olive oil
- 1/2 teaspoon dried thyme
- 1/2 teaspoon dried oregano
- 1/2 cup rolled oats
- 1/2 cup all purpose flour
- Salt, pepper (to taste)

DIRECTIONS:
1. Preheat oven to 375 degrees. Sauté leeks in a large frying pain for 5-8 minutes until tender and allow to cool.
2. Steam the cauliflower approximately 15 minutes, until tender. In a large mixing bowl, mash the cauliflower. Combine with the rest of the ingredient list.
3. Line a 13×9 baking pan with parchment paper. Wet hands and form mixture into a burger shape, and evenly distribute in pan. Bake for 30-40 minutes, until golden brown.

Bean and Garlic Burgers

Servings	6-8 burgers

INGREDIENTS:
- 2 garlic heads
- 2 onions, chopped
- 3 cups canned white beans, drained and rinsed
- 3 tablespoons olive oil
- 1 teaspoon dried thyme
- 1 teaspoon smoked paprika
- 1 cup cooked quinoa
- 2 tablespoons all purpose flour
- Salt, pepper (to taste)

DIRECTIONS:
1. Preheat oven to 350 degrees. Sauté onions and olive oil for 8-10 minutes in large frying pan.
2. Wrap garlic in tin foil and bake until tender. Scoop flesh into a large mixing bowl.
3. Pulse beans and garlic in food processor until smooth. Place mixture back into mixing bowl and add the remaining ingredient list, combine well.
4. Line a 13×9 baking pan with parchment paper. Wet hands and form mixture into a burger shape, and evenly distribute in pan. Bake for 30-40 minutes, until golden brown.

Chickpea Soy Sauce Burgers

Servings	8–10 burgers

INGREDIENTS:

- 1 cup canned chickpeas, drained
- 2 cups canned white beans, drained
- 1 cup tempeh, crumbled
- 1 teaspoon cumin
- 1 tablespoon soy sauce
- 2 tablespoons tahini paste
- 2 green onions, chopped
- 3/4 cup rolled oats
- Salt, pepper (to taste)

DIRECTIONS:

1. Preheat oven to 350 degrees. In a food processor, combine chickpeas and beans until well blended, but still chunky. Place mixture in a large mixing bowl, and combine with crumbled tempeh, cumin, soy sauce, tahini paste, green onions, rolled oats, and salt/pepper.

2. Line a 13×9 baking pan with parchment paper. Wet hands and form mixture into a burger shape, and evenly distribute in pan. Bake for 30–40 minutes, until golden brown.

Rosemary Mushroom Burgers

Servings	4 burgers

INGREDIENTS:
- 4 large, stuffing mushrooms
- 4 oz tofu
- 1 teaspoon soy sauce
- 1 green onion, chopped
- 1/2 teaspoon dried oregano
- 1/2 teaspoon dried basil
- 1/4 teaspoon dried rosemary
- Salt, pepper (to taste)

DIRECTIONS:
1. Preheat oven to 350 degrees. In a large mixing bowl, crumble the tofu and add ingredient list, minus the mushrooms, until well blended.
2. Line a 13×9 baking pan with parchment paper. Scoop mixture from bowl into mushrooms, and evenly distribute in pan. Bake for 20-30 minutes, until golden brown.

Coriander Sunflower Seed Burgers

Servings	8-10 burgers

INGREDIENTS:
- 2 cups cooked red lentils, drained
- 2 cups canned white beans, drained
- 1 onion, finely chopped
- 3 tablespoons sunflower seeds
- 1/2 cup rolled oats
- 1 teaspoon cumin
- 1/2 teaspoon dried oregano
- 1 tablespoon flax seeds, ground
- 2 tablespoons water
- Salt, pepper (to taste)

DIRECTIONS:
1. Preheat oven to 350 degrees. Combine flax seeds and water and let soak ten minutes.
2. In a food processor, pulse beans until paste forms. Place bean mixture in large mixing bowl and combine with cooked lentils, onion, seeds, oats, cumin, oregano, flax seeds, and salt/pepper.
3. Line a 13×9 baking pan with parchment paper. Wet hands and form mixture into a burger shape, and evenly distribute in pan. Bake for 30-40 minutes, until golden brown.

Bean Burgers

Black Bean Burgers with Sour Cream and Lime

Servings	4 burgers

INGREDIENTS:
- 2 dried Chipotle Peppers
- 1 cup Red Onions, chopped
- 1/2 cup Carrots, chopped
- 1 cup Mushrooms, chopped
- 1 cup frozen Corn Kernels, thawed
- 1/4 cup chopped fresh Italian Parsley
- 1 tsp Cumin, ground
- 1/4 tsp Cider Vinegar
- 1 can Black Beans, rinsed and drained
- 1/4 cup blue or yellow Cornmeal
- 1/3 cup unseasoned dry Bread Crumbs

To make the Tofu Sour Cream:
- 1 pack Silk Tofu (12 oz)
- 2 tbsp Extra Virgin Olive Oil
- 1 tsp Agave nectar
- 2 tbsp Freshly Squeezed Lemon Juice
- 1/4 tsp Salt

To make the Lime Cream Sauce:
- 1/3 cup Tofu Sour Cream
- 1 tbsp Lime Juice
- 1/4 tsp Chili Powder
- Hot Pepper Sauce

DIRECTIONS:

To make the tofu sour cream:

1. Puree all ingredients together until well blended.

To make the lime cream:

1. Combine all ingredients in a small mixing bowl.

To make the burgers:

1. Put peppers in a small glass bowl, cover completely with boiling water and let set for ten minutes, drain. Discard stems and seeds, finely chop pepper.

2. In a large frying pan, sauté carrots, onions, and olive oil on medium until soft. Add peppers, mushrooms, corn, parsley, vinegar and cumin, cook five minutes and remove from heat.

3. In a large mixing bowl, mash the beans with a wooden spoon. Add cornmeal and vegetable mixture until well combined.

Bean Burgers

Pumpkin Black Bean Burgers

Servings	6 burgers

INGREDIENTS:

To make the patty:
- 2 cans Black Beans, rinsed and drained
- 2 Carrots, grated
- 1/2 cup Rolled Oats
- 1/4 cup Pumpkin Seeds
- 1 tbsp Olive Oil
- 1/2 tsp Cinnamon
- 1/2 tsp Cumin
- 1/2 tsp Coriander
- 1/2 tsp Chili Powder
- 1/2 tsp Onion Powder
- 1/4 tsp Cayenne Pepper
- 1 tsp Salt
- 1/4 tsp Black Pepper

To make the ketchup:
- 1 cup Tomato Puree
- 1/2 cup Vegetable Broth
- 2 tbsp Lemon Juice
- 1 tbsp Balsamic Vinegar
- Pinch of Salt
- Dash of Pepper
- Dash of Garlic Powder

DIRECTIONS:

To make the ketchup:

1. Puree all ingredients in a food processor until smooth. Add more seasonings if necessary.

To make to burgers:

1. Preheat oven to 300 degrees. Coarsely mix pumpkin seeds and oats in a food processor. Add carrots, 3 cups of the beans, all spices and olive oil. Mix well using the pulse setting.

2. Add mixture to a large mixing bowl and fold in the remaining beans.

3. With wet hands, form mixture into burger shape and evenly distribute on a baking sheet. Bake for 40 minutes, turning once after 20 minutes.

Jalapeno Lima Bean Burgers

Servings	8 burgers

INGREDIENTS:

To make the patty:
- 1 can Lima Beans, drained
- 1 Onion, finely chopped
- 1 tbsp Jalapeno Pepper, finely chopped
- 6 Saltine Crackers, crushed
- 1 Flax Egg
- 1/4 tsp Garlic Powder
- 1 tsp of salt
- 1 tsp of Pepper
- 1/4 cup Olive Oil

To make the Ketchup:
- 1 to 2 Tomatoes
- 1/2 cup Sun Dried Tomatoes
- Pinch of Salt
- 3 Dates
- Water or Lemon Juice, only as needed

To make a Flax: (egg substitute)
- 1 tbsp ground, raw Flax Seeds (or Chia Seeds, healthier but more expensive)
- 3 tbsp Cold Water

DIRECTIONS:

To make the Flax:

1. Combine flax and water in a small mixing bowl. Refrigerate 15-60 minutes, until mixture is sticky and glue like.

To make the ketchup:

1. In a food processor, combine all ingredients until smooth in texture.

To make the burgers:

1. In a large mixing bowl, mash lima beans with fork. Add entire rest of ingredient list and flax from the refrigerator. Mix until combined well.

2. Using wet hands, mold the mixture into a burger shape. Put a tablespoon of olive oil in a large frying pan and put over medium heat. Fry each side of patty for five minutes, cooking until both sides are golden brown in color.

Freekeh and Harissa Burgers

Servings	4-6 burgers

INGREDIENTS:

To make the patty:
- 1 1/2 cup Pinto Beans, cooked
- 1 Flax Egg
- 1/2 cup cracked Freekeh, cooked according to package instructions
- 2 cloves Garlic, minced
- 1/4 cup Carrots, shredded
- 1/4 cup Green Onions, sliced
- 1 tbsp Zapata
- 1 tsp Cumin
- Salt/Pepper (to taste)
- 1 tbsp Olive Oil
- 1 large Onion, sliced thinly
- 1 to 2 tsp Harissa
- 1 batch of Smoky Garlic Aioli

To make the smoky garlic aioli:
- 3/4 cup raw Cashews, soaked in water for 4 to 8 hours
- 1 clove Garlic
- 1/4 cup and 2 tbsp Water
- 2 tbsp Lemon Juice
- 1/2 tsp Smoked Paprika
- Salt/Pepper (to taste)

To make the Flax Egg:
- 1 tbsp ground, raw Flax Seeds (or Chia Seeds)
- 3 tbsp Cold Water

DIRECTIONS:

To make the Flax Egg:

1. Combine flax seeds and water, refrigerate for 15-60 minutes. It is ready to be used in recipe when it is sticky and glue like.

To make the smoky garlic aioli:

1. Drain/Rinse cashews. Combine all ingredients in food processor, adding water if necessary.

To make the burgers:

1. Preheat oven to 350 degrees. In a large mixing bowl, mash beans using a wooden spoon, leaving beans chunky.

2. Mash beans in a large bowl using a masher or wooden spoon, but not completely. Add the rest of the ingredient burger list to the mixing bowl, as well as the flax seed egg and mix well.

3. With wet hands, mold the mixture into a burger shape. Evenly place the burgers on a un-greased baking sheet. Rub olive oil on top side of burger. Bake 20-25 minutes until golden brown.

4. In a large frying pan, sauté the onions with olive oil until golden brown. Add the harissa, in increments to your desired spice level.

5. Layer burger with onion mixture and aioli. Enjoy

Bean Burgers

White Burger with Tomato

Servings	4 burgers

INGREDIENTS:

To make the burgers:
- 1 can Cannellini beans, rinsed and drained
- 1 1/2 cup Breadcrumbs
- 1/4 cup Carrot, shredded
- 1/4 cup Onion, chopped
- 1 Flax Egg
- 2 tbsp Fresh Parsley
- 3 tbsp Olive Oil, divided
- 1 cup Baby Spinach

To make the tomato sauce:
- 1 oz Tomato, diced
- 2 tbsp Fresh Basil
- Salt/Pepper (to taste)

To make the Flax Egg:
- 1 tbsp ground, raw Flax Seeds (or Chia Seeds)
- 3 tbsp Cold Water

DIRECTIONS:

To make the Flax Egg:
1. Combine flax seeds and water. Refrigerate 15-60 minutes, until mixture is sticky and glue like.

To make the tomato sauce:
1. Pulse tomato in food processor until smooth. Combine other ingredients.

To make the burgers:

1. In a large mixing bowl, mash the beans with a wooden spoon. Combine with half of the bread crumbs, carrot, onion, flax egg, half of the parsley, one tablespoon oil and salt/pepper.
2. In a separate bowl combine remainder of bread crumbs and parsley.
3. Form mixture into burger shape using wet hands. Place burgers in bread crumb mixture and coat both sides evenly. Add remaining olive oil to a large frying pan and cook burgers until golden brown on both sides, approximately four minutes on each side.

Scallion Potato Burgers

Servings	4 burgers

INGREDIENTS:

To make the burgers:
- 1 cup canned Black Beans
- 1 Carrot, grated
- 1/2 Onion, diced
- 3 Potatoes, grated
- 4 Scallions, chopped
- 1 cup Corn
- Pinch of Salt
- Dash of Ground Black Pepper
- 2 tbsp Extra Virgin Olive Oil

To make Vegan Mayonnaise
- 1 cup Olive or Canola Oil
- 1/2 cup Soy Milk
- 1 tsp Lemon Juice, fresh
- Pinch of Salt
- Pinch of Ground Mustard

DIRECTIONS:

To make the vegan mayo:

1. Put soy milk and lemon juice in blender and combine for approximately 30 seconds. Thicken mixture by slowly adding in the olive oil. Once desired thickness, add mustard and salt, as needed.

To make the burgers:

1. Mash the beans with a fork in a large mixing bowl. Add remaining ingredients from burger list, minus the olive oil, until well combined.

2. Wet hands and form burger shape with the mixture. On medium heat, in a large frying pan, cook burgers for five minutes on each side.

Cornmeal Crusted Black Bean Burgers

Servings	6 burgers

INGREDIENTS:

To make the burgers:
- 2 cans Black Beans, rinsed and drained
- 1/2 cup Whole Wheat or all-purpose flour
- 1/4 cup yellow Cornmeal
- 2 tsp Cumin, ground
- 1 tsp Garlic Salt
- 6 Whole Wheat Buns

To make the salsa
- 1 big fresh Tomatoes, chopped finely
- 1 Onion, chopped finely
- 3 mild Chili, chopped finely
- Bunch of Coriander, chopped finely
- Pinch of Salt
- Lime Juice, to taste
- 1 tbsp Water

DIRECTIONS:

To make the salsa:
1. Combine all ingredients in a medium sized bowl.

To make the burgers:
1. Pulse beans in a food processor until smooth, but still slightly chunky.
2. In a large bowl, combine all ingredients in large mixing bowl until well blended.

3. With wet hands, form mixture into a burger shape. Put grill on medium. Grill each burger for five minutes on each side, until golden brown.

Cilantro Bean Burger

Servings	4 burgers

INGREDIENTS:

To make the burgers:
- 1/2 can of Black Beans, drained and rinsed
- 1 can of red Kidney Beans
- 2 tbsp. White Onion, minced
- 1/2 cup Corn, thawed
- 1/2 cup Whole Wheat Breadcrumbs
- 1/2 tsp Cumin, ground
- 1/2 tsp Coriander, ground
- 1/3 cup chopped Cilantro
- 4 tbsp. Hot Sauce
- 4 Buns, lightly toasted
- 1 Flax Egg
- Mixed greens
- 1 Avocado, mashed
- Pinch of Salt

To make the Flax Egg
- 1 tbsp ground, raw Flax Seeds (or Chia Seeds)
- 3 tbsp Cold Water

DIRECTIONS:

To make the Flax Egg:
1. Combine water and flax seed. Put in refrigerator 15-60 minutes, until sticky and glue like.

To make the burgers:

1. In a large mixing bowl, mash the beans with a potato masher. Combine with chopped onions, breadcrumbs, corn, cilantro, two tbsp. hot sauce, flax egg and a pinch of salt.

2. With wet hands, form mixture into a burger shape. In a large frying pan with oil, heated to medium temperature, Cook each side of the burger approximately four minutes, until brown and crispy.

3. Mash the avocado and spread on favorite bun and add favorite burger toppings.

Mushroom Garlic Burgers

Servings	6 burgers

INGREDIENTS:

To make the burgers:
- 1 can Black Beans, drained and rinsed
- 1 1/2 cups diced Mushrooms
- 1/2 cup plain rolled Oats
- 2 cloves Garlic, chopped
- 1 Flax Egg
- 1 tbsp Cumin
- 1/4 tsp Black Pepper, ground
- 2 tsp Olive Oil
- 6 Whole Grain Buns
- 6 tbsp Spicy Mustard
- 1 Tomato, sliced
- 1 cup Baby Spinach

To make the Flax Egg
- 1 tbsp ground, raw Flax Seeds (or Chia Seeds)
- 3 tbsp Cold Water

DIRECTIONS:

To make the Flax Egg:
1. Combine flax seeds and water, refrigerate for 15-60 minutes until sticky and glue like.

To make the burgers:
1. Preheat grill - medium. Pulse half the beans in a food processor, combining with mushrooms, oats, garlic, egg, cumin, and pepper. Combine well.

2. Place remaining beans in processor and continue to pulse until smooth.
3. With wet hands, mold mixture into burger shape. Grill each side of burger for four minutes, until golden brown.
4. Burgers taste best with toasted burgers and choice of toppings, some listed in list.

Chili Powder Oat Burgers

Servings	8 burgers

Ingredients:

To make the burgers:
- 1 Onion, minced
- 1 tbsp Tomato Ketchup
- 2 tbsp Tamari or Liquid Amino
- 2 tbsp Dijon Mustard
- 1 1/2 cups Quick-Cook Oats
- 1/2 cup dry Pinto Beans
- 1/2 cup dry Black Beans
- 1 tsp Cumin, ground
- 1 1/2 tsp Chili Powder
- 1 Carrot, grated
- 4 cloves Garlic, finely chopped

To make the Ketchup:
- 1 to 2 Tomatoes
- 1/2 cup Sun Dried Tomatoes
- Pinch of Salt
- 3 Dates
- Water or Lemon Juice, only as needed

Directions:

To make the ketchup:
1. Combine all ingredients in a food processor until smooth in texture.

To make the burgers:

1. Cover beans with cold water and soak approximately 2-3 hours. Cook beans until tender.
2. In a large frying pan, sauté onion and garlic for approximately two minutes. Add carrots, chili powder, and cumin and cook until carrot is tender. Allow to cool.
3. In a large mixing bowl, mash the beans with a potato masher. Add carrot mixture and remaining ingredient list for the burger. Combine well
4. With wet hands, form mixture into a burger shape. Add oil to a large frying pan and cook burgers on medium heat, approximately five minutes on each side.

Mexican Sliders

Servings	12 burgers

INGREDIENTS:

To make the burgers:
- 1/4 cup Extra Virgin Olive Oil
- 1 yellow Onion, diced
- 1 can Black Beans, drained and rinsed
- 1/4 cup Carrots, diced
- 1/4 cup Corn
- 1/4 cup Red Bell Pepper, chopped
- 1/4 cup Spinach, chopped
- 1/2 cup Cornmeal
- 1/2 cup Breadcrumbs
- Pinch of Sea Salt
- 1/2 cup Salsa Verde
- 12 Slider Buns of your choice
- 1 Avocado, pitted
- 1/2 cup vegan Mayonnaise
- 1 clove of Garlic, finely chopped

To make vegan mayonnaise:
- 1 cup Olive Oil
- 1/2 cup Soy Milk
- 1 tsp Lemon Juice, fresh
- Pinch of Salt
- Pinch of Ground Mustard

DIRECTIONS:

To make the vegan mayo:

1. In a blender, combing soy milk and lemon juice. Continue blending, slowly pouring in the olive oil. Once at desired thickness, add salt and mustard.

To make the burgers:

1. Sauté onion in a large frying pan with two tablespoons of olive oil, using medium heat until caramelized, approximately twenty minutes. Chop vegetables in ingredient list while the onions are caramelizing.

2. In a large mixing bowl, combine caramelized onions, black beans, carrots, spinach, black pepper corn, cornmeal, breadcrumbs, sea salt, and salsa verde.

3. With wet hands, form mixture into burger shape. In a large frying pan, heat olive oil on medium heat. Cook burgers on each side approximately two minutes, until golden brown.

4. Make the topping for your burger by whisking avocado, vegan mayonnaise and garlic together in a medium mixing bowl.

Chipotle Sweet Potato Burgers

Servings	6-8 burgers

INGREDIENTS:

To make the burgers:
- 1 medium Sweet Potato, baked and peeled
- 16oz. cooked White Beans (canned, drained and rinsed)
- 1/2 cup White Onion, finely chopped
- 2-3 tbsp Tahini
- 3/4 tsp Apple Cider Vinegar
- 1 tsp Garlic Powder
- 1/2 - 1 tsp Chipotle Powder
- 1/2 tsp Salt
- 1/4 tsp Black Pepper
- 1/3 cup Nutritional Yeast OR any Flour
- 1/2 - 1 cup finely chopped Greens (kale, spinach, parsley)
- 1 tbsp Extra Virgin Coconut Oil

To garnish:
- 1 medium Avocado, peeled, pitted and sliced horizontally
- 6 slices Tomato
- 6 Whole-wheat Buns

For the Vegan Mayonnaise:
- 1 cup Olive Oil
- 1/2 cup Soy Milk
- 3/4 tsp Salt
- Pinch of Ground Mustard
- 1 to 1 1/2 tsp Lemon Juice

DIRECTIONS:

To make the vegan mayonnaise:

1. Blend all ingredients, minus the lemon juice in a blender. Slowly pour the lemon juice in blender until mixture thickens. Add salt if necessary.

To make the burgers:

1. Preheat oven to 400 degrees. Wrap sweet potato with foil and cook approximately forty minutes, until tender.
2. In a large mixing bowl, mash potato and beans. Add entire rest of ingredient list for burger and combine well.
3. Heat coconut oil in large frying pan over medium heat. With wet hands, form the mixture into a burger shape. Cook each side of burger until golden brown in color.

Black Beans & Oat Burgers

Servings	8 burgers

INGREDIENTS:

To make the burgers:
- 1/2 cup Onion, diced
- 1 large Garlic Clove, finely chopped
- 1 Flax Egg
- 1 cup Oats, processed into Flour
- 1 1/2 cup Bread Crumbs
- 1 cup minced Carrots
- 1 cup Black Beans, cooked and rinsed and mashed
- 1/4 cup Parsley, minced
- 1/3 cup Almonds, chopped
- 1/2 cup Sunflower seeds
- 1 tbsp Extra Virgin Olive Oil
- 1 tbsp Tamari or Liquid Amino
- 1 1/2 tsp Chili Powder
- 1 tsp Cumin
- 1 tsp Oregano
- Pinch of Salt
- Dash of Black Pepper

To make the Flax Egg:
- 1 tbsp ground, raw Flax Seeds (or Chia Seeds)
- 3 tbsp Cold Water

DIRECTIONS:

To make the Flax Egg:

1. Combine flax seeds with water and refrigerate for 15-60 minutes until sticky and glue like.

To make the burgers:

1. Preheat oven to 350 degrees. Put a tablespoon of olive oil in a large frying pan and sauté garlic and onion.
2. Put onion mixture, flax egg, and all ingredients, except spices and salt, into a large mixing bowl, combine well, add spices and mix.
3. Wet your hands and form mixture into burger shape. Evenly distribute in a 13×9 baking dish, bake for 25-30 minutes, flipping after 15 minutes, cooking until golden and crispy.

Chickpea Burgers

Sweet Potato Cilantro Burgers with Peanut Sauce

Servings	6–8 burgers

INGREDIENTS:

To make the burgers:
- 1 large Sweet Potato (peeled)
- 1/2 cup Cilantro, chopped
- 1/4 cup Basil Leaves, chopped
- 3 cloves Garlic, minced
- 2 tsp Ginger, grated
- 3/4 cup Rolled Oats, processed into a coarse flour
- 1 can Chickpeas, drained and rinsed
- 2 tbsp Ground Flax mixed with 3 tbsp Water in a bowl
- 1/2 tbsp Sesame Seed Oil
- 1 tbsp Liquid Amino
- 1 tsp Fresh Lime Juice
- 1 tsp Ground Coriander
- 1 tsp Salt
- A dash of ground Black Pepper

For making the peanut sauce:
- 1 clove Garlic
- 6 tbsp Smooth Peanut Butter
- 2 1/2 tbsp Fresh Lime Juice
- 2 tbsp Liquid Amino
- 1 to 2 tbsp Water
- 1/2 tbsp Maple Syrup

- 1 tsp Ginger, freshly grated
- 1/8 tsp Cayenne Pepper

DIRECTIONS:

To make the peanut sauce:

1. Pulse all ingredients in a food processor until smooth in texture.

To make the burgers:

1. Preheat oven to 350 degrees. Line a 13×9 baking dish with parchment paper.
2. Grate 1.5 cups of the sweet potato. Put in a large mixing bowl, combine with cilantro, basil, garlic, and ginger.
3. In a large bowl, add the grated sweet potato, cilantro, basil, garlic, and ginger. Mix well.
4. In a food processor, pulse the oats until a flour like texture is formed. Mix oats with sweet potato mixture.
5. In food processor, pulse chickpeas until ground, not paste. Add chickpeas to sweet potato mixture and combine.
6. Combine flax seed and water and let set for one minute, add to bowl once thickened.
7. Combine rest of ingredients with mixture.
8. Wet hands and mold mixture into a burger shape. Place burgers onto baking sheet and cook forty minutes, flipping after twenty minutes. Both sides should be golden brown.

Cajun Burgers

Servings	12 burgers

INGREDIENTS:

To make the burgers:
- 1 tbsp Olive Oil
- 1/4 cup Onion, diced
- 1/4 cup Green Pepper, diced
- 1 stalk Celery, diced
- 1 can (28 oz) Chickpeas, rinsed and drained
- 1 tsp Thyme
- 1 tsp Paprika
- A pinch of Cayenne Pepper
- 1 tsp Hot Sauce
- 2 tbsp Fresh Parsley, chopped
- 2 tbsp Flour
- 1 tbsp Cornstarch
- A pinch of Salt
- A dash of Pepper

To make the Ketchup:
- 1 to 2 Tomatoes
- 1/2 cup Sun Dried Tomatoes
- Pinch of Salt
- 3 Dates
- Water or Lemon Juice, only as needed

DIRECTIONS:

To make the ketchup:

1. Combine all ingredients using a food processor until smooth.

To make the burgers:

1. Heat oil in frying pan on medium heat. Add onion, green pepper, and celery to pan and cook until tender, approximately five minutes.

2. Put chickpeas and frying pan mixture into a food processor and combine until coarse. Add all ingredients, minus the flour and cornstarch and combine well. Mix in the flour and cornstarch and put bowl in refrigerator for thirty minutes.

3. After thirty minutes, form the mixture into burger shape using wet hands. Warm frying pan again over medium heat and cook burgers for three minutes on each side, or until golden brown and crispy.

Curry Peanut Butter Burgers

Servings	6 burgers

INGREDIENTS:
- 1 1/2 cup cooked Chickpeas
- 1/2 cup rolled Oats
- 1/3 cup Chick Pea Flour
- 3 cloves Garlic, finely chopped
- 1 tsp Cumin
- 1 tsp Curry Powder
- 1 tsp Ground Black Pepper
- 1/2 tsp Baking Soda
- 2 tbsp Lemon Juice
- 1 tbsp natural Peanut Butter
- 3 to 4 Kale Leaves, remove stems and finely chopped
- Pepitas, handful
- Sunflower seeds, handful
- Raisins, handful
- 2 tbsp extra virgin olive oil

DIRECTIONS:
1. Pulse chickpeas in food processor until paste forms. Add paste and remaining ingredient list into large mixing bowl, minus one tablespoon of olive oil, and combine well.
2. With wet hands, form mixture into a burger shape and sprinkle patties with flour.
3. Warm a large frying pan with one tablespoon of olive oil over medium heat. Cook both sides approximately five minutes, until golden brown.

Cilantro Zucchini Burgers

Servings	8 burgers

INGREDIENTS:

To make the burgers:
- 1 can Chickpeas, drained, rinsed and mashed
- 1/2 red Onion, finely diced
- 1 small Zucchini, grated
- 3 tbsp Cilantro, finely chopped
- 3 tbsp Red Wine Vinegar
- 1 tbsp Sirracha Sauce
- 2 tbsp Natural Peanut Butter
- 1 tsp Cumin
- 1 tsp Garlic Powder
- 2 tsp Black Pepper
- 1/2 tsp Sea Salt
- 1 cup quick Oats
- 2 tbsp Olive Oil

To make vegan mayonnaise:
- 1 cup Olive Oil
- 1/2 cup Soy Milk
- 1 tsp Lemon Juice, fresh
- Pinch of Salt
- Pinch of Ground Mustard

Chickpea Burgers

DIRECTIONS:

To make the vegan mayonnaise:

1. Blend soy milk and lemon juice in blender for thirty seconds. Slowly drizzle oil into mixture until desired thickness. Add seasonings.

To make the burgers:

1. Preheat oven to 400 degrees. In a large bowl add all burger ingredients and combine.

2. With wet hands, mold mixture into a burger shape. Place in a greased 13×9 baking dish. Bake for forty minutes, flipping burgers after twenty minutes. Each side should be golden brown.

Lentils

Mushroom Lentil Burgers

Servings	4 burgers

INGREDIENTS:

To make the burgers:
- 1 cup dried Green Lentils
- 2 1/4 cups Water
- 1 tsp dried Parsley
- 1/4 tsp Black Pepper
- 3 Garlic cloves, minced
- 1 1/4 cups Onion, finely chopped
- 3/4 cup Walnuts, finely chopped
- 2 cups fine Bread Crumbs
- 1/2 cup Flax Seed, ground
- 3 cups Mushrooms, finely chopped
- 1 1/2 cups Spinach, stems removed and finely chopped
- 2 tbsp Coconut Oil
- 3 tbsp Balsamic Vinegar
- 2 tbsp Dijon Mustard
- 2 tbsp nutritional Yeast
- 1 tsp Sea Salt
- 1/2 tsp Black Pepper
- 1/2 tsp Paprika

To make the Ketchup:
- 1 to 2 Tomatoes
- 1/2 cup Sun Dried Tomatoes
- Pinch of Salt
- 3 Dates
- Water or Lemon Juice, only as needed

DIRECTIONS:

To make the ketchup:

1. In a food processor, combine all ingredients until smooth.

To make the burgers:

1. In a large saucepan, bring to a boil: lentils, water, parsley, 1 garlic clove, and 1/4 cup of onion. After one minute, reduce to simmer and cook for 35-40 minutes, partially covered, until water is absorbed.

2. While the lentil mixture is simmering, combine walnuts, bread crumbs, and flax seed in a bowl. Add yeast, paprika, and salt/pepper, combine.

3. In a large frying pan, sauté remaining onion, remaining garlic, mushrooms, and greens with one tablespoon of olive oil for approximately ten minutes. Allow to cool.

4. Once lentils are cooked, put them in a large mixing bowl, add vinegar and mustard, mash mixture with a wooden spoon. Add frying pan mixture and bread crumb mixture and combine. Refrigerate for thirty minutes.

5. Using wet hands, mold mixture into a burger shape. In a large frying pan, heat one tablespoon of olive oil over medium heat. Cook burgers for five minutes on each side, or until golden brown and crispy.

Cumin Carrot Burger

Servings	6 burgers

INGREDIENTS:
- 1/2 cup dried Green Lentils, rinsed
- 1/2 cup brown rice
- 1 Onion, chopped
- 1 Carrot, grated
- 4 Garlic cloves, minced
- 3 tsp Cumin, ground
- 1 tsp Sage, ground
- 1 tsp Sea Salt
- 1 1/2 cup Water
- 1 cup Vegetable Broth

To make the Ketchup:
- 1 to 2 Tomatoes
- 1/2 cup Sun Dried Tomatoes
- Pinch of Salt
- 3 Dates
- Water or Lemon Juice, only as needed

DIRECTIONS:

To make the ketchup:
1. Put all ingredients in a food processor, and blend until smooth.

To make the burgers:
1. Add all ingredients to a large saucepan and bring to a boil. Reduce heat to simmer and cook for forty minutes, until rice is tender. Drain if necessary and allow to cool.

2. Once cooled, place mixture into food processor and pulse until smooth in texture. Wet hands and mold mixture into a burger shape. Heat grill to medium, brush burgers with olive oil and grill on each side for five minutes. Burgers are ready when crispy around the edges.

Brown Rice Burgers

Servings	8 burgers

INGREDIENTS:
- 1 cup Lentils, uncooked
- 1 cup Brown Rice, uncooked
- 1 to 1/2 cups Carrots, finely chopped
- 1/2 tsp Garlic Powder
- 1 to 1/2 cups uncooked Oatmeal
- 1 tsp Season Salt
- 1 small Onion, finely chopped

DIRECTIONS:

1. Bring to a boil: rice, lentils and 4 cups water/vegetable broth in a large saucepan, boil for one minute, reduce heat to simmer and cover for forty five minutes. Allow to cool.

2. In a large mixing bowl, add rice mixture and entire ingredient list, combine.

3. Wet hands and form mixture into burger shape. In a large frying pan, add one tablespoon of olive oil and cook burgers for five minutes on each side on medium heat, until golden brown in color.

Mushroom Burgers

Mushroom with Garlic Mayonnaise

Servings	2 burgers

INGREDIENTS:

To make the burgers:
- 2 large Portobello Mushroom Caps, cleaned and stem removed
- 2 tbsp Olive Oil
- 1 clove Garlic, minced
- 1 tsp dried Thyme
- 2 slices fresh ripe Tomatoes
- 1/2 red onion, finely chopped
- 1/2 tsp pepper
- Salt to taste

To Make Vegan Mayonnaise:
- 1 cup Olive Oil
- 1/2 cup Soy Milk
- 1 tsp Lemon Juice, fresh
- Pinch of Salt
- Pinch of Ground Mustard

To Make the Garlic Mayonnaise:
- 2 tbsp of the Vegan Mayo
- 1 tsp Lemon Juice
- 1 clove Garlic, minced
- 2 tbsp Bermuda Onions, minced
- 1/2 tsp dried Thyme, minced
- 1/2 tbsp dried Parsley, minced

Directions:

To make the vegan mayonnaise:

1. Blend soy milk and lemon juice for thirty seconds in blender. Slowly add olive oil, blending until desired thickness. Season as necessary.

To make the garlic mayonnaise:

1. In a small mixing bowl, combine all ingredients. Refrigerate thirty minutes.

To make the burgers:

1. In a medium mixing bowl, combine two tablespoons olive oil, minced garlic cloves, onion, thyme, salt and pepper. Soak the mushrooms in mixture for forty five minutes.

2. Add one tablespoon of olive oil to a large frying pan over medium heat. Place each of the mushrooms into the frying pan along with the mixture they soaked in. Cook mushroom on each side for five minutes.

Potato, Portobello, Peach Burgers

Servings	6 burgers

INGREDIENTS:

To make the burgers:
- 6 Portobello Mushrooms
- 6 Peaches
- 6 Sweet Potatoes
- 6 Whole Wheat Buns of your choice
- 1/2 cup fresh Pea Sprouts
- 5 small roman Tomatoes, sliced
- 5 small spring Onions, sliced
- Fresh Thyme
- Olive Oil
- Pinch of Salt
- 1/2 tbsp Pepper, ground

To make the Marinade:
- 4 tbsp Olive Oil
- 2 fresh Rosemary Sprigs
- 1 tbsp fresh Thyme
- 2 Garlic cloves
- 1/2 Lemon
- Pinch of Salt
- Dash of Pepper

To make the Guacamole:
- 4 avocados
- 5 small Roma Tomatoes
- 1 Garlic clove

- 1/4 cup Parsley
- 1/2 Lemon
- 1 tbsp Olive Oil

DIRECTIONS:

To make the guacamole:

1. Dice avocado and tomatoes, chop parsley. In a small mixing bowl, add garlic, avocado, tomato, and parsley. Drizzle with lemon juice and mash with a fork.

To make the marinade:

1. In a small mixing bowl, pour the olive oil. Chop one rosemary sprig and thyme, add garlic, freshly squeezed lemon juice and salt/pepper to taste. Combine well.

To make the burgers:

1. Wash the mushrooms. Spoon peaches into each. Dip unused rosemary sprig into marinade and brush the mushrooms and peaches.

2. Use the remaining rosemary sprig to brush the mushrooms and peaches with the marinade. Heat grill to medium heat and grill mushrooms on each side for 4 minutes each. Once flipped, brush marinade over mushroom again with sprig.

Mushrooms Black Bean Burgers

Servings	8 burgers

INGREDIENTS:

To make the burgers:
- 2 cups Portabella Mushrooms
- 2 cups cooked Black Beans, rinsed and divided
- 1 cup fresh Broccoli, minced
- 1/2 cup Red Onion, minced
- 3 Flax Eggs
- 1/2 cup plus 2 tbsp Panko Breadcrumbs
- 1 tbsp Montreal Steak Seasoning
- 1 tbsp Vegan Worcestershire
- 2 tbsp Garlic, minced
- Olive Oil

To make Worcestershire Sauce:
- 1/2 cup Apple Cider Vinegar
- 2 tbsp Soy Sauce or Liquid Amino
- 2 tbsp Water
- 1 tbsp Brown Sugar
- 1/4 tsp Ground Ginger
- 1/4 tsp Dry Mustard
- 1/4 tsp Onion powder
- 1/4 tsp Garlic powder
- 1/8 tsp Cinnamon powder
- 1/8 tsp Pepper

For 3 Flax Eggs:
- 3 tbsp ground, raw Flax Seeds (or Chia Seeds)
- 9 tbsp Cold Water

DIRECTIONS:

To make Worcestershire Sauce:

1. Cook all ingredients in a large saucepan, on medium heat. Stir frequently until boiling, Reduce heat to simmer, stirring continuously for one minute and remove from heat. Allow to cool and store in refrigerator.

To make the Flax Eggs:

1. Combine flax seeds and water. Refrigerator for 15-60 minutes, until mixture is sticky and glue like.

To make the burgers:

1. In a large bowl, mash one cup black beans with a potato masher. Add remaining ingredients, minus breadcrumbs and flax egg. Combine well. Gently stir in the breadcrumbs and flax egg.

2. Add one tablespoon of olive oil to a large frying pan and heat on medium With wet hands, form mixture into a burger shape. Cook each side of the burger for five minutes, until golden brown in color.

Crimini Lentil Onion Burger

Servings	6 burgers

INGREDIENTS:

To make the burgers:
- 1 clove Garlic, chopped
- 1 cup Cremini Mushrooms, remove stems
- 1 tbsp fresh Thyme Leaves
- 2 tbsp Olive Oil, divided
- 1 Onion, chopped
- 1 cup canned Lentils, drained and rinsed
- 3/4 cup Whole-Wheat Breadcrumbs
- 1 Flax Egg
- 1 tsp Salt
- 1/2 cup Yellow Cornmeal
- 6 Whole-grain Buns
- 8 Tomato slices
- Basil Leaves, fresh

To make the Flax Egg
- 1 tbsp ground, raw Flax Seeds (or Chia Seeds)
- 3 tbsp Cold Water

DIRECTIONS:

To make the Flax Egg:
1. Combine flax seed and water. Place in refrigerator for 15-60 minutes. Mixture is ready to use when it is sticky and glue like.

To make the burgers:

1. Pulse garlic, crimini mushrooms and fresh thyme leaves in a food processor until finely chopped.

2. Sauté onion and one tablespoon of olive oil in a large frying pan until the onion is a golden brown. Add chopped ingredients from food processor and cook until liquid evaporates. Allow to cool.

3. Combine frying pan mixture with remaining ingredient list (minus the cornmeal)in a large mixing bowl, combine well. With wet hands, form mixture into burger shape. Coat burgers on each side with cornmeal.

4. In a large frying pan, add one tablespoon of olive oil and heat to medium. Cook each side of burger until golden brown in color, approximately three minutes.

Vegetable Burgers

Hummus Eggplant Burger

Servings	2 burgers

INGREDIENTS:
- 4 slices Eggplant, thick
- 2 tbsp Olive Oil
- 1/2 tsp Paprika
- 1/2 tsp Garlic powder
- 1/2 tsp Salt
- 1/4 tsp Pepper
- 2 tsp Oregano

DIRECTIONS:

1. Put eggplant slices on cutting board and generously sprinkle with salt, allow to set for thirty minutes. Pat dry with a paper towel.

2. In a large mixing bowl, combine olive oil, garlic powder, paprika, oregano and salt/pepper. Brush the mixture onto both sides of the eggplant.

3. Set the grill to medium heat and cook each side of eggplant for three minutes.

Broccoli Scallion Burgers with Tahini

Servings	4 burgers

INGREDIENTS:

To make the burgers:
- 1/3 cup Dry Couscous
- 1 cup Water
- 1 1/2 cups Broccoli florets
- 2 tsp Olive Oil
- 1/2 cup Scallions, chopped
- 1/2 cup Yellow Onion, chopped
- 2 tsp Ground Cumin
- 1 can (15 oz) Chickpeas, rinsed and drained
- 1 tbsp Sesame Tahini
- 1/2 cup Panko Breadcrumbs

To make the Tahini dressing:
- 1/3 cup Sesame Tahini
- 1/3 cup Water
- 1/4 cup and 1 tbsp Fresh Lemon Juice
- 2 cloves Garlic, chopped
- ¾ tsp Salt

DIRECTIONS:

To make the tahini sauce:
1. Pulse all ingredients in a food processor, until well blended.

To make the burgers:
1. Preheat oven to 400 degrees. In a large saucepan, boil water and couscous. Boil for one minute and set aside, allowing couscous to soak in the water for a minimum of ten minutes.

Vegetable Burgers

2. Steam broccoli for seven minutes, until tender. Sauté scallions and onion in a large frying pan for approximately five minutes, on medium heat. Remove from heat, add cumin and combine.

3. Put couscous, broccoli, onion mixture, sesame tahini, and chickpeas into food processor and pulse until well mixed. Put the food processor mixture into a large mixing bowl and add breadcrumbs.

4. Using wet hands, mold the mixture into burger shape. Line a baking sheet with aluminum foil and evenly distribute the burgers. Bake for fifty minutes, flipping burger after twenty five minutes. Both sides should have a golden brown color.

Spinach Burger with Vegan Cheese

Servings	12 burgers

INGREDIENTS:

To make the burgers:
- 10 ounces frozen Spinach, chopped
- 1 Potato
- 1 Onion
- 1 Bell Pepper
- 1 cup frozen Green Beans, French-style cut
- 1 tbsp Garlic Powder
- 1 tbsp dried Onions, chopped
- 1/2 tsp. Paprika
- 1/2 cup BBQ Sauce
- 1/2 cup Bread Crumbs
- 1 1/2 cup quick rolled Oats
- 1/2 tsp Salt
- 1 tsp Vegetable Broth Powder

To make Vegan Yeast Cheese:
- 1/4 cup nutritional Yeast Flakes
- 1/4 cup unbleached White Flour
- 1/2 tsp Sea Salt
- 1/4 tsp Garlic Powder
- 1 cup water
- 1 tbsp Tahini
- 1/4 tsp prepared Mustard

Vegetable Burgers

DIRECTIONS:

TO MAKE VEGAN YEAST CHEESE:

1. Combine dry ingredients in a large saucepan and add water. Cook on medium until mixture thickens and starts to boil. Continually whisk mixture during cooking. Once boiling, boil for thirty seconds and remove from heat. Add in tahini and mustard, combine and chill in refrigerator approximately fifteen minutes.

TO MAKE THE BURGERS:

1. Thaw frozen spinach in microwave, allow to cool. Stab potato multiple times with a knife, and microwave potato for seven minutes. Once cool enough to touch, peel and dice potato.

2. Dice green pepper and onion. Place in microwave safe dish, cover with 1/8 cup of water, cover with plastic wrap. Poke a few holes in plastic to vent and microwave for six minutes.

3. In a large mixing bowl, combine all ingredients. With wet hands, mold the mixture into a burger shape. In a large frying pan, cook on medium heat in one tablespoon of olive oil until burger is crispy on each side.

Chili Potato Burger

Servings	12 burgers

INGREDIENTS:

To make the burgers:
- 1/2 Grated Cauliflower head
- 1 Potato, boiled and mashed
- 1/4 cup Onion, chopped
- 3 tbsp Cilantro, finely chopped
- 3/4 tsp Salt
- 1/2 tsp Kashmiri Garam Masala
- 1 tsp Whole Coriander Seeds
- 1/2 Green Chili, finely chopped
- 1 Tomato
- 2 cloves of Garlic
- 1/2 inch Ginger, pulsed to a paste
- 1 tbsp Olive Oil
- Flour as needed

For the breadcrumb coating:
- 1/2 cup Breadcrumbs
- 1/4 tsp black pepper
- 1/2 tsp salt
- 1/2 tsp garlic powder

To make vegan mayonnaise
- 1 cup Olive Oil
- 1/2 cup Soy Milk
- 1 tsp Lemon Juice, fresh
- Pinch of Salt
- Pinch of Ground Mustard

Vegetable Burgers

DIRECTIONS:

To make the vegan mayo:

1. Blend soy milk and lemon juice in blender for thirty seconds. Slowly pour in olive oil until desired thickness. Season to taste.

To make the breadcrumb coating:

1. On a large serving plate, combine all ingredients.

To make the burgers:

1. Preheat oven to 365 degrees. In a large mixing bowl, combine all ingredients on the list until combined. Add enough flour to make the burgers less moist and mold into burger shape.

2. Evenly coat both sides of burger with the breadcrumb coating. Evenly distribute burgers on a greased baking sheet. Drizzle oil over the top.

3. Bake for approximately forty minutes, flipping after twenty. Burgers are done when both sides are crispy and golden brown.

Red Pepper Spinach Burgers

Servings	5 burgers

INGREDIENTS:

To make the burgers:
- 6 oz Spinach, finely chopped
- 2 Flax Eggs
- 1 Onion, chopped
- 1/2 cup Bread Crumbs
- 2 cloves Garlic, minced
- 1 tsp Olive Oil
- 1 tsp Red Pepper Flakes
- 1/2 tsp Salt

To make the Ketchup:
- 1 to 2 Tomatoes
- 1/2 cup Sun Dried Tomatoes
- Pinch of Salt
- 3 Dates
- Water or Lemon Juice, only as needed

To make 2 Flax Eggs
- 2 tbsp ground, raw Flax Seeds (or Chia Seeds)
- 6 tbsp Cold Water

DIRECTIONS:

To make the Flax Eggs:
1. Combine flax seed and water. Refrigerate 15-60 minutes until mixture is sticky and glue like.

Vegetable Burgers

To make the ketchup:

1. Put all ingredients in food processor and blend until smooth.

To make the burgers:

1. In a large frying pan, sauté onions and garlic until translucent, approximately five minutes.

2. In a large mixing bowl, combine spinach, salt, red pepper flakes, flax eggs, and garlic and onion well.

3. Mix in the breadcrumbs until mixture becomes sticky. With wet hands, mold burger into burger shape.

4. In a large frying pan, add one tablespoon of olive oil and heat to medium. Cook each side of burger for three minutes, until golden brown color and crispy.

Burgers and Fries

Servings	5 burgers

INGREDIENTS:

To make the patties
- 1 Yam, peeled and cut into chunks
- 2/3 cup Onion, sliced
- 1 Red Bell Pepper
- 4 Dates
- 5 tbsp Ground Flax Seeds
- 4 tbsp Nutritional Yeast
- 4 large Mushrooms
- 4 cloves Garlic
- 1/4 tsp Salt
- 1/4 tsp Pepper
- 1/4 tsp Cumin
- 1/4 tsp Coriander
- 1/4 tsp Cinnamon
- 1/4 tsp Basil
- 1/4 tsp Turmeric
- 1/4 tsp Paprika

To make the Fries:
- 1 Daikon Radish, peeled and cut into fries
- 1 tsp Olive Oil
- 1/4 tsp Salt
- 1/4 tsp Pepper
- 1/4 tsp Cumin
- 1/4 tsp Coriander

Vegetable Burgers

- 1/4 tsp Cinnamon
- 1/4 tsp Basil
- 1/4 tsp Turmeric
- 1/4 tsp Paprika

To make the Ketchup:
- 1 to 2 Tomatoes
- 1/2 cup Sun Dried Tomatoes
- Pinch of Salt
- 3 Dates
- Water or Lemon Juice, only as needed

To assemble the burger:
- 10 raw vegan bread slices, for 5 tops and bottoms
- Tomato slices
- Lettuce
- Sliced onion

DIRECTIONS:

To make the ketchup:

1. Using a food processor, blend all ingredients until smooth.

To make the patties:

1. Preheat oven to 425 degrees. Cut the vegetables into hearty chunks. Put all ingredients for burgers into food processor and pulse until well blended, but still chunky.

2. With wet hands, mold mixture into burger shape. Evenly distribute burgers on a greased baking sheet and bake twenty minutes, flipping burgers after ten minutes. Burgers are done when they are crispy along the edges.

To make the fries:

1. Combine oil and seasonings, rub on radishes. Spread evenly on baking sheet and bake for forty minutes.

Mixed Vegetables Burger

Servings	4 burgers

INGREDIENTS:

- 1 1/2 cup Sweet Potato, peeled and chopped
- 1 small Carrot, peeled and grated
- 1 small Zucchini, grated
- 1/4 cup Corn Kernels
- 1/4 cup Peas
- 2 Green Onions, chopped
- 1 Flax Egg
- 1/2 cup Plain Flour
- 2 tsp Olive Oil
- 4 Multigrain Bread Rolls
- 1/4 cup Baby Spinach
- 2 tbsp Sweet Chili Sauce

To make the Flax Egg
- 1 tbsp ground raw Flax Seeds
- 3 tbsp Cold Water

DIRECTIONS:

To make the Flax Egg:

1. Combine flax seed and water, refrigerate for 15-60 minutes until mixture is sticky and glue like.

To make the burgers:

1. In a large saucepan bring water to boil, put sweet potato and a dash of salt into water and turn heat to medium. Cook 8 to 10 minutes, until tender. Drain and let cool.

Vegetable Burgers

2. In a large mixing bowl, mash the sweet potato. Add carrots, corn, peas, zucchini, onion, flax egg, and flour combine.
3. With wet hands, mold mixture into a burger shape. In a large frying pan, heat one tablespoon of olive oil on medium-high. Cook patties until golden brown and crispy, approximately five minutes on each side.

Grain, Nut and Seed Burgers

Quinoa, Chili Powder Burgers

Servings	8 burgers

INGREDIENTS:

To make the burgers:
- ¾ cup Quinoa, cooked
- 1/2 cup Red Onion, finely chopped
- 1 cup Mushroom, finely chopped
- Pinch of Salt & Black Pepper
- 1 15-ounce can Black Beans, well rinsed and drained
- 1 cup raw Beet, finely grated
- 1 tsp Cumin
- 1 tsp Chili Powder
- 1 tsp Paprika, smoked
- 1/2 raw Walnuts, crushed

To make Worcestershire Sauce:
- 1/2 cup Apple Cider Vinegar
- 2 tbsp Soy Sauce or Liquid Amino
- 2 tbsp Water
- 1 tbsp Brown Sugar
- 1/4 tsp Ground Ginger
- 1/4 tsp Dry Mustard
- 1/4 tsp Onion powder
- 1/4 tsp Garlic powder
- 1/8 tsp Cinnamon powder
- 1/8 tsp Pepper

To make mayonnaise:
- 1 cup Olive Oil
- 1/2 cup Soy Milk
- 1 tsp Lemon Juice, fresh
- Pinch of Salt
- Pinch of Ground Mustard

DIRECTIONS:

To make the mayonnaise:

1. Blend soy milk and lemon juice in blender for thirty seconds. Slowly add olive oil until desired thickness. Season to your own taste.

To make Worcestershire Sauce:

1. Put all ingredients in a medium saucepan and put over medium heat. Once boiling stir constantly, reduce heat to simmer for 1 minute, Allow to cool and put in refrigerator to chill.

To make the burgers:

1. Preheat oven to 375 degrees. Add one tablespoon of olive oil to a large frying pan and put on low heat. Sauté onion for about 5 minutes, until translucent.

2. In a large mixing bowl, combine black beans and onions, mash with a potato masher. Add the quinoa, beet and spices, combine. Stir in the walnuts, mix well.

3. With wet hands, mold mixture into a burger shape and evenly distribute in a greased 13×9 baking dish. Bake 40 minutes, flipping after twenty.

Lemon Bell Pepper Burger

Servings	4 burgers

INGREDIENTS:

To make the burgers:
- 1/2 cup Quinoa
- 1 cup Water
- 1 tsp Garlic powder
- 3 tsp Thyme, divided
- 1 tsp Smoked Paprika
- 1 can White Beans, rinsed and drained
- 1/2 cup Corn
- 1/2 cup Red Bell Pepper, finely diced
- 1/2 cup Shallots, finely diced
- juice of 1 Lemon
- 1/3 cup Flour
- Dash of Pepper
- Pinch of Salt
- Olive Oil for greasing

For the garnish:
- 4 slices of Tomatoes
- 4 slices of Red Onion
- Dijon mustard

DIRECTIONS:

1. Preheat oven to 375 degrees. In a large saucepan, bring water, quinoa, garlic powder and one teaspoon thyme to a boil. Cover and reduce heat to simmer, cook fifteen minutes. Let cool for ten minutes before using.

2. Mash beans in a large mixing bowl. Dice corn, shallots, and red pepper to the size of a pea. Put vegetables in the large mixing bowl. Add remaining burger ingredients, as well as quinoa mixture and combine.

3. With wet hands, mold mixture into a burger shape. Distribute on ungreased baking dish and bake for forty minutes, flipping after twenty.

Lentil Quinoa Burgers

Servings	6 burgers

INGREDIENTS:

To make the burgers:
- 1/2 cup Quinoa
- 1 can Lentils, rinsed
- 1/2 cup plain Bread Crumbs
- 1 Flax Egg
- 2 gloves Garlic, chopped
- 2 tsp Cumin Powder
- 1/3 cup Cilantro
- Lemon Juice, half
- 1/2 cup Walnut pieces
- 1 tbsp Tahini
- 1 cup Crimini Mushrooms, sliced
- 1/4 cup dry Red Wine
- 2 tsp Vegetable Oil
- 6 Whole Grain Buns

To make the Flax Egg
- 1 tbsp ground, raw Flax Seeds (or Chia Seeds)
- 3 tbsp Cold Water

DIRECTIONS:

To make the Flax Egg:
1. Combine flax seed and water. Refrigerator for 15-60 minutes, until mixture is sticky and glue like.

To make the burgers:

1. In a large saucepan, combine quinoa and one cup water. Bring to a boil over medium-high heat, boil one minute, lower heat and simmer for ten minutes. Allow to cool.
2. In a large mixing bowl, combine half the lentils, breadcrumbs, flax egg, garlic, cumin, cilantro, lemon juice, quinoa, and salt/pepper.
3. Put mixture in a food processor, add remaining lentils and walnuts, pulse until well combined.
4. With wet hands, mold mixture into burger shape. Turn grill on to medium heat.
5. In a large frying pan, melt tahini on medium heat, add sliced mushrooms and sauté for five minutes. Add wine and continue to sauté for five more minutes.
6. Brush burgers with olive oil, grill for six minutes on each side, until golden brown.

Chive Burgers

Servings	12 burgers

INGREDIENTS:

To make the burgers:
- 2 1/2 cups Quinoa, cooked
- 4 Flax Eggs
- 1/2 tsp Salt
- 1/3 cup Fresh Chives, finely chopped
- 1 White Onion, finely chopped
- 3 Cloves Garlic, finely chopped
- 1 cup whole grain bread crumbs
- Water, if needed
- 1 tbsp Olive Oil

To make 4 Flax Egg:
- 4 tbsp ground, raw Flax Seeds (or Chia Seeds)
- 12 tbsp Cold Water

To make the Ketchup:
- 1 to 2 Tomatoes
- 1/2 cup Sun Dried Tomatoes
- Pinch of Salt
- 3 Dates
- Water or Lemon Juice, only as needed

DIRECTIONS:

To make the Flax Egg:
1. Combine flax seeds and water and refrigerate for 15-60 minutes, until mixture becomes sticky and glue like.

To make the ketchup:

1. Blend all ingredients in a food processor until smooth.

To make the burgers:

1. In a large mixing bowl, combine quinoa, flax eggs and salt. Add chives, cloves and garlic, combine. Stir in the breadcrumbs and wait for moisture to be absorbed.

2. With wet hands, mold mixture into burger shape. In a large frying pan, cook burgers in one tablespoon of olive oil on medium heat for seven minutes on each side, until golden brown.

Tomato Spinach Burgers

Servings	7 burgers

INGREDIENTS:

To make the burgers:
- 4 Sun-dried Tomatoes, not packed in oil
- 1 1/2 cup Vegetable Broth
- 1/2 cup Millet, rinsed
- 1/4 tsp Salt
- 6 tsp Extra Virgin Olive Oil, divided
- 1 large Onions, chopped
- 3 cups Baby Spinach, stems trimmed
- 2 cloves Garlic, minced
- 1 tbsp Fresh Basil, chopped
- 2/3 cup Fine Dry Breadcrumbs
- 1/4 tsp Pepper, freshly ground
- 7 whole-wheat buns or whole-wheat English muffins
- Arugula, for garnish
- Sliced tomatoes, for garnish

To make the Olive Ketchup
- 1/2 cup pitted Kalamata Olives
- 1/4 cup Fresh Parsley, chopped
- 1 clove Garlic, crushed and peeled
- 1 tbsp Extra Virgin Olive Oil
- 1 tsp Red Wine Vinegar
- 2 tsp Tomato Paste

DIRECTIONS:

To make the olive ketchup:

1. In a food processor, blend all ingredients, minus the tomato paste. Transfer into a small mixing bowl, stir in tomato paste.

To make the burgers:

1. In a small saucepan, cover the sun dried tomatoes with water. Bring tomatoes to a boil and remove from heat. Allow to soak for thirty minutes, drain.

2. In a medium saucepan, bring broth to a boil. Add millet and a dash of salt, boil for one minute. Reduces heat to low and cover, simmering for twenty minutes. Remove from heat and leave at room temperature for twenty minutes.

3. In a large frying pan, heat two teaspoons of olive oil to temperature on medium heat. Cook onion for seven minutes, until golden brown. Add spinach and cook until leaves wilt. Add garlic and cook for one more minute. Put mixture on large serving plate and let cool for ten minutes.

4. In a food processor, pulse millet. Add spinach mixture, pulse until finely chopped. Put mixture in a large mixing bowl; combine with basil, bread crumbs, pepper and sun-dried tomatoes.

5. Using wet hands, mold mixture into a burger shape. In a large frying pan, cook patties on medium heat with one tablespoon of olive oil for approximately four minutes on each side.

Grain, Nut and Seed Burgers

Spicy Mustard Buckwheat Burgers

Servings	4 burgers

INGREDIENTS:

To make the burgers:
- 1 cup Toasted Buckwheat
- 2 Carrots, grated
- A handful of fresh Parsley, chopped
- 1 tsp Dried Basil
- 1 tsp Dried Thyme
- 1/2 tsp Dried Oregano
- 1 tsp Paprika
- 1/2 tsp Mustard powder, ground
- 1/4 to 1/2 tsp Cayenne pepper (depending on how spicy you want it)
- A dash of Pepper
- A pinch of Salt

To make the guacamole:
- 4 pieces Hass Avocado, peeled, seeded and cut into chunks
- 1 tbsp Lemon Juice
- 1/2 small White Onion, minced
- 1 piece Roma Tomato, seeded and diced
- A dash of Pepper
- A pinch of Salt

DIRECTIONS:

To make the guacamole:
1. In a medium mixing bowl, mash the avocado and lemon juice with a fork. Combine with the remaining guacamole ingredients.

To make the burgers:

1. In a large saucepan, bring to a boil: roasted buckwheat, a dash of salt and two cups water. Boil for one minute, reduce heat to simmer and cook for fifteen minutes. Add carrots, parsley and spices.

2. Using wet hands, mold the mixture into a burger shape. Turn the grill on medium heat. Grill each side of burger until golden brown and crispy, approximately 5-7 minutes on each side.

Walnut Rice Burgers

Servings	10 burgers

INGREDIENTS:

To make the burgers:
- 2 cups instant Brown Rice
- 1 ¾ cups low-sodium Vegetable Broth
- 1/2 Onion, finely chopped
- 1 Carrot, finely chopped
- 2 cloves Garlic
- 1 1/4 cups Walnuts
- 2 Flax Eggs
- 1/2 cup Sesame Seeds Paprika
- Pinch of Salt
- Dash of Pepper
- 10 reduced-calorie Hamburger Buns
- 10 slices Tomato
- 10 Lettuce Leaves

To make 2 Flax Eggs:
- 2 tbsp ground, raw Flax Seeds (or Chia Seeds)
- 6 tbsp Cold Water

DIRECTIONS:

To make the Flax Egg:
1. Combine flax seed and water in a small mixing bowl. Place mixture into refrigerator for 15-60 minutes, until mixture is sticky and glue like.

To make the burgers:

1. In a large saucepan, bring to a boil (medium-high): rice, broth, onion, carrot, and garlic. Turn heat down to simmer and cook five minutes, cover and remove from heat to set for five minutes. Spread mixture onto baking sheet.

2. In a food processor, pulse walnuts until finely chopped. Add rice mixture and flax egg and combine until mixture is sticky.

3. Using wet hands, mold mixture into burger shape. Salt/pepper to taste and sprinkle with paprika. Evenly coat the burgers with sesame seeds on both sides.

4. In a large frying pan, cook burgers in olive oil on medium heat for four minutes on each side, until golden brown and crispy.

Nutty Oat Burger

Servings	11 burgers

INGREDIENTS:

To make the burgers:
- 1 tbsp finely grated raw beet
- 1/2 cup cooked Oats (quick or regular rolled oats)
- 1 cup uncooked oats (quick or regular rolled oats)
- 1/2 cup walnuts, coarsely ground
- 1/4 cup almonds, coarsely ground
- 2 tbsp Sesame Seeds
- 1 tbsp Vegetable broth
- 1/4 cup Green Pepper, minced
- 1/4 cup Celery, minced
- 1/4 cup Onion, minced
- 1 tsp dried basil
- 1/4 tsp dried thyme
- 1/4 tsp dried thyme
- 1/4 tsp ground sage
- 1/4 tsp mustard powder
- 2 tbsp Soy Sauce (Liquid Amino or Tamari)

To make mayonnaise:
- 1 cup Olive Oil
- 1/2 cup Soy Milk
- 1 tsp Lemon Juice, fresh
- Pinch of Salt
- Pinch of Ground Mustard

DIRECTIONS:

To make the mayonnaise:

1. Blend soy milk and lemon juice for thirty seconds, slowly add olive oil until desired thickness, season to taste.

To make the burgers:

1. In a large mixing bowl, combine all ingredients.
2. Using wet hands, mold mixture into burger shape. Heat grill to medium heat and add burgers, cooking each side until golden brown and crispy.

Peanut Butter Oat Burgers

Servings	4 burgers

INGREDIENTS:
- 1 Onion
- 1 cup raw Nut of choice
- 1 cup Rolled Oats, raw
- 2 tbsp Ketchup
- 2 tbsp Miso
- 2 tbsp Tomato Paste
- 2 tbsp Peanut Butter
- 1 tsp Chili Powder
- Pinch of Salt
- Dash of Black Pepper, freshly ground
- 1 Flax Egg
- 2 tbsp Peanut Oil
- Extra Virgin Olive Oil

To make the Ketchup:
- 2 Tomatoes
- 1/2 cup Sun Dried Tomatoes
- Pinch of Salt
- 3 Dates
- Water or Lemon Juice, only as needed

To make the Flax Egg:
- 1 tbsp ground, raw Flax Seeds (or Chia Seeds)
- 3 tbsp Cold Water

DIRECTIONS:

To make the ketchup:

1. In a food processor, blend all ingredients until smooth.

To make the Flax Egg:

1. Combine flax seeds and water. Refrigerator for 15-60 minutes, until mixture becomes sticky and glue like.

To make the burgers:

1. In a food processor, finely mince the onions. Add nuts and oats, and combine until coarse. Add all other ingredients except oil and blend well. Add a little water to mixture if it becomes to dry.

2. With wet hands, mold mixture into burger shape. In a large frying pan, add one tablespoon olive oil and heat to medium. Cook burgers on each side for five minutes.

Grain, Nut and Seed Burgers

Raisin Walnut Burger

Servings	10 burgers

INGREDIENTS:
- 1 cup Walnut
- 2 Carrots, chopped
- 1/2 Onion, chopped
- 1/2 tbsp Raisins
- 1/2 tbsp Olive Oil
- 1/2 tbsp Salt
- 1/2 tbsp Pepper
- Sprinkle of Paprika

DIRECTIONS:

1. In a food processor, coarsely chop the walnuts. Place all other ingredients into food processor and blend for two minutes to combine.

2. Using wet hands, mold mixture into burger shape. Sprinkle with paprika. In a large frying pan, on medium heat, cook burgers with one tablespoon of olive oil for five minutes on each side, until crispy around the edges.

Seitan

Smoky Garlic Celery Burger

Servings	8 burgers

INGREDIENTS:
- 2 tsp Chipotle Chili in Adobo Sauce (canned)
- 1/2 cup Whole Wheat Bread Flour
- 1/4 cup Yellow Cornmeal
- 1 1/2 tsp Medium-Hot Chili Powder
- 1 tsp Cumin, ground
- 1/4 tsp Ground Pepper
- 1/2 cup Barbecue Sauce
- 12 oz Seitan
- 1 tbsp Olive Oil
- 1 cup Onion, finely chopped
- 3 cloves Garlic, minced
- 1/2 cup Green Bell Pepper, finely chopped
- 1/2 cup Shiitake Mushrooms, stemmed and finely chopped
- 1 tsp Salt
- 1/4 tsp Dried Oregano
- 1/4 tsp Dried Thyme
- 1/4 tsp Celery Seed
- 1/4 tsp Dry Mustard
- 1/4 tsp Ginger, ground

DIRECTIONS:
1. Drain seitan and place in food processor, pulse until coarse.
2. Sauté onion in a large frying pan with olive oil until golden brown. Add to onion: garlic, green pepper, mushrooms, oregano, 1/2 teaspoon salt, thyme, celery seed, ginger, cayenne and mustard. Cook for at least five minutes.

3. Add frying pan ingredients to a large mixing well. Add seitan and chipotle, combine.

4. In a medium mixing bowl, add flour, cornmeal, cumin, chili powder, remaining 1/2 teaspoon salt and pepper. Slowly add this mixing bowl's contents to the large mixing bowl until combined.

5. Using wet hands, mold mixture into a burger shape. Preheat gas grill to high and place burgers on grill. Brush barbecue sauce onto top side, cook for five minutes. Flip burgers, again brush with barbecue sauce and cook another five minutes.

Caper Burgers with Paprika

Servings	6 burgers

INGREDIENTS:

To make the burgers:
- 1 1/4 Vital wheat Gluten
- 1/4 cup Nutritional Yeast
- 1 cup Vegetable Stock
- 1/2 cup White Beans such as Cannellini
- 1 tbsp Tomato Ketchup
- 2 tbsp Olive Oil
- 2 tbsp Soy Sauce (or Liquid Amino)
- 1 tbsp Capers, finely chopped
- 1 Garlic, crushed
- 1 tbsp Herbes de Provence
- 1/2 Smoked Paprika
- Black Pepper

To make the Ketchup:
- 1 to 2 Tomatoes
- 1/2 cup Sun Dried Tomatoes
- Pinch of Salt
- 3 Dates
- Water or Lemon Juice, only as needed

DIRECTIONS:

To make the ketchup:
1. Put all ingredients in a food processor and blend until smooth.

To make the burgers:

1. Preheat oven to 200 degrees. In a large mixing bowl, add beans and mash with fork.

2. Add to the beans: stock, ketchup, olive oil, soy sauce, capers and garlic, combine.

3. In a medium mixing bowl: add vital wheat gluten, yeast, herbs, pepper and paprika, combine. Combine both bowls and knead with hands to combine.

4. Cut mixture into 6 even pieces. Roll the burger into a ball and place on baking sheet lines with aluminum foil. Bake meatballs approximately 20 minutes until crisp.

Soy

Nutty Soy Burgers with Ketchup

Servings	20 burgers

INGREDIENTS:

To make the burgers:
- 2 cups dry Soybeans, cooked in 4 cups of water in slow cooker set on low for 12 hours
- 5 raw Carrots, peeled
- 1 cup Brazil Nuts
- 1/2 cup Tamari
- 1 tbsp dried Parsley
- 1 tbsp dried Basil
- 3 cups Wheat Germ

To make the Ketchup:
- 1 to 2 Tomatoes
- 1/2 cup Sun Dried Tomatoes
- Pinch of Salt
- 3 Dates
- Water or Lemon Juice, only as needed

DIRECTIONS:

To make the ketchup:
1. In a food processor, blend all ingredients until smooth.

To make the burgers:
1. Preheat oven to 400 degrees and line baking sheet with aluminum foil, apply cooking spray.

2. Combine soybeans and carrots in food processor until smooth. Add brazil nuts and pulse until beans are coarsely chopped. In a large mixing bowl, combine this mixture with Tamari. Add parsley, basil, and wheat germ, combine.

3. With wet hands, mold mixture into a burger shape and even distribute on baking sheet. Bake for thirty minutes, flipping after fifteen.

Sesame Tofu Burger

Servings	6 burgers

INGREDIENTS:
- 2 cups Tofu
- 1/2 cup Whole Wheat Flour
- 3 tbsp Nutritional Yeast
- 2 tbsp Vegetable Bouillon Powder Pepper
- 2 tbsp Tamari or Liquid Amino
- 1/4 cup Sesame Seeds
- 1 small Potato, scrubbread
- 1/4 tsp Garlic powder
- Onion Powder

To make mayonnaise:
- 1 cup Olive Oil
- 1/2 cup Soy Milk
- 1 tsp Lemon Juice, fresh
- Pinch of Salt
- Pinch of Ground Mustard

DIRECTIONS:

To make the mayonnaise:
1. In a blender, combine soy milk and lemon juice for thirty seconds. Slowly add olive oil to mixture until desired thickness. Season to taste.

To make the burgers:
1. Preheat oven to 350 degrees. Pulse tofu in food processor, until coarse. Add remaining ingredients and combine.

2. Using wet hands, mold mixture into burger shape and evenly distribute on a baking sheet lined with tin foil. Bake for 30–45 minutes, until golden brown and crispy.

Sauerkraut Burger

Servings	6 burgers

INGREDIENTS:

To make the Burger:
- 1 1/3 cup Hot Water
- 1 cup TVP (Texturized Vegetable Protein)
- 1/2 cup Onion, minced
- 1 1/2 cup Vital Wheat Gluten
- 1/2 cup Dill Pickle Juice
- 2 tbsp Tomato Paste
- 1 tbsp Canola Oil
- 1 1/2 cups Sauerkraut, heated

To make the Thousand Island dressing:
- 1 cup Veganaise
- 1/3 cup Ketchup
- 1/2 tsp Onion Powder
- A dash of Salt
- 3 tbsp Sweet Pickle Relish

To make the Reuben Spice Blend:
- 1 tbsp Coriander, ground
- 2 tsp Allspice, ground
- 2 tsp Garlic powder
- 2 tsp Onion powder
- 2 tsp Paprika
- 1/2 tsp Caraway Seeds, ground
- 1/4 tsp Fennel Seeds, ground
- 1/4 tsp Black Pepper, ground

DIRECTIONS:

To make the Reuben spice blend:

1. In a small mixing bowl, add all ingredients listed for spice blend and combine.

To make the Thousand Island dressing:

1. In a small mixing bowl, add all dressing ingredients and combine until smooth.

To make the burgers:

1. In a large mixing bowl, add water and TVP and soak for approximately ten minutes, until TVP is dehydrated. Add onion, vital wheat gluten, and Reuben spice blend, combine by using a fork.

2. Add pickle juice, tomato sauce and oil to the same large mixing bowl. Knead mixture with hands until well combined.

3. Cut six pieces of aluminum foil into twelve inch squares. Evenly distribute burger mixture onto these twelve pieces of foil. Flatten the mixture to form burger shape, and wrap in tin foil, leaving room for the burger to expand during cooking.

4. Put the burgers in a steamer for about an hour.

Gravy TVP Burgers

Servings	3 burgers

INGREDIENTS:

To make the burgers:
- 1 Vegex cube (or vegetable bouillon)
- 1 tsp Spike seasoning
- 1/2 tsp Onion powder
- 1 tsp Gravy Master
- ¾ cup boiling Water
- 1 cup dry TVP
- 1 small Onion, diced
- 1 tbsp Oil
- 1/2 tsp Chili Powder
- 1/4 tsp Garlic Powder
- Pinch of Black Pepper
- 1/2 tsp Oregano
- 1 tbsp Tamari or Liquid Amino
- 1/4 cup White Flour

To make the Ketchup:
- 1 to 2 Tomatoes
- 1/2 cup Sun Dried Tomatoes
- Pinch of Salt
- 3 Dates
- Water or Lemon Juice, only as needed

DIRECTIONS:

To make the ketchup:

1. In a food processor, blend all ingredients until smooth.

To make the burgers:

1. In a large saucepan: pour boiling water, vegex, spike, onion powder and gravy master.

2. Add the TVP and cover for 10 minutes. Sauté onion in a small frying pan and add to TVP mixture.

3. Add chili powder, garlic, pepper, oregano and liquid amino (or tamari) to TVP mixture, stir flour into saucepan until combined.

4. With wet hands, mold mixture into a burger shape. On medium-high heat, warm olive oil in a large frying pan, cook burgers in pan for five minutes on each side, until golden brown and crispy.

Super Combo Burgers

Barbecue Brown Rice Burger

Servings	8 burgers

Ingredients:
- 1 can Garbanzo Beans, drained and mashed
- 8 Basil Leaves, freshly minced
- 1/4 cup Oat bran
- 1/4 cup quick cooking Oats
- 1 cup cooked Brown Rice
- 1 pack Tofu
- 5 tbsp barbecue Sauce
- 1/2 tsp Salt
- 1/2 tsp Black Pepper, ground
- 3/4 tsp Garlic Powder
- 3/4 tsp dried Sage
- 2 tsp Olive Oil

Directions:
1. Combine mashed beans and basil leaves in a large mixing bowl. Add oat bran, quick oats, and rice, combine.
2. In a medium mixing bowl, squeeze excess water from tofu. Add barbecue sauce to bowl and toss to coat.
3. Add tofu mixture to bean mixture, combine. Stir in salt, pepper, sage, and garlic powder until combined. Wet hands and form mixture into burger shape.
4. Heat one tablespoon of olive oil in a large frying pan on medium heat. Cook burgers on each side for five minutes, until both sides are crispy around the edges.

Mexican Style Burgers

Servings	4 burgers

INGREDIENTS:

To make the burgers:
- 2 ounces Olive Oil
- 3 tbsp red Onion, diced
- 2 tbsp Black Olives, diced
- 2 tbsp red Bell Peppers, diced
- 1 tsp Jalapeno, diced
- 1 1/2 tbsp Garlic, diced
- 1 tbsp Artichoke, diced
- 4 oz Black Beans, drained
- 4 oz Chickpeas, drained
- 4 oz White Beans, drained
- 6 oz Rolled Oats
- 1/2 tsp Hungarian Paprika
- 1/2 tsp Chili Powder
- 1 tsp dried Oregano
- 1 tbsp fresh Parsley Leaves, minced
- 1/2 tsp red Chili Flakes
- 1/2 tsp cumin, ground
- 1/2 tsp Celery Salt
- 1/4 tsp Sage, ground
- 2 tbsp seasoned Bread Crumbs
- 1 Flax Egg

To make Mayonnaise:
- 1 cup Olive Oil
- 1/2 cup Soy Milk

Super Combo Burgers

- 1 tsp Lemon Juice, fresh
- Pinch of Salt
- Pinch of Ground Mustard

To make the Flax Egg:
- 1 tbsp ground, raw Flax Seeds (or Chia Seeds)
- 3 tbsp Cold Water

DIRECTIONS:

To make the Flax Egg:

1. Combine flax seeds and water. Put in refrigerator for 15-60 minutes, until mixture becomes sticky and glue like.

To make the mayonnaise:

1. In a blender, combine soy milk and lemon juice for approximately thirty seconds. Slowly add olive oil until desired thickness. Season to taste.

To make the burgers:

1. Add one tablespoon of olive oil to a large frying pan and warm to medium heat. Add all vegetables listed in burger ingredient list, except for beans. Sauté five minutes.
2. Once vegetable mixture has cooled, add to beans in a large mixing bowl, combine. Add all other dry ingredients listed and flax egg, combine.
3. Using wet hands, form mixture into a burger shape. In the large frying pan used to sauté the vegetables, reheat pan to medium heat and cook burgers for three minutes on each side. Burgers are done when they are golden brown on each side.

Zucchini Apple Burger

Servings	4 burgers

INGREDIENTS:

To make the burgers:
- 1/2 cup cracked Wheat
- 1/4 lb Green Beans
- 1 Zucchini
- 1 Carrot, peeled
- 1/2 Granny Smith Apple, peeled
- 1/2 cup canned Chick Peas, rinsed and drained
- 1 tbsp Onion, minced
- 1 tbsp Sesame Tahini or peanut butter
- 1/2 tbsp Canola Oil
- 1/2 tsp Curry Powder
- 1/2 tsp Chili Powder
- 1/2 tsp Salt
- Black Pepper, ground
- 1/2 cup Bread Crumbs

To make Mayonnaise:
- 1 cup Olive or Canola Oil
- 1/2 cup Soy Milk
- 1 tsp Lemon Juice, fresh
- Pinch of Salt
- Pinch of Ground Mustard

Super Combo Burgers

DIRECTIONS:

To make the mayonnaise:

1. In blender, combine soy milk and lemon juice for thirty seconds. Slowly add olive oil to blender until desired thickness. Season to taste.

To make the burgers:

1. In a medium saucepan, add water and green beans. Boil until beans are tender. Chop finely.

2. In a large saucepan, boil one cup water, cook cracked wheat by boiling approximately one minute. Remove wheat from burner and cover.

3. In a large mixing bowl, grate zucchini, carrot, and apple. After grating, squeeze excess moisture out with cheesecloth or dish towel. Combine vegetable mixture with chopped green beans.

4. In a food processor, pulse chickpeas, onions, garlic, tahini, curry powder, chili powder, salt, pepper, and canola oil until smooth in texture. Add to mixing bowl with grated vegetable mixture.

5. Pour cracked wheat into strainer, use a wooden spoon to remove excess water from wheat by pressing against sides of strainer. Add wheat and breadcrumbs to vegetable mixture, combine. Refrigerate for one hour.

6. Using wet hands, mold mixture into a burger shape. Cook on a grill, each side for three minutes, until golden brown in color.

BONUS RECIPE:

PURPLE BURGER

INGREDIENTS:
- 3/4 cup cooked quinoa
- 1/2 large red onion, finely diced (3/4 cup)
- 1 cup finely chopped mushrooms (shitake, baby bella or white button)
- Salt & Pepper
- 1 15-ounce can black beans, well rinsed and drained
- 1 cup finely grated raw beet
- 1 tsp cumin
- 1/2 tsp chili powder (or sub extra cumin)
- 1/4 tsp smoked paprika
- 1/2 cup raw walnuts, crushed or ground into a loose meal

INSTRUCTIONS:
1. Heat a large skillet over medium-low heat and add a bit of olive oil. Once hot add the onion and sauté, seasoning with a pinch each salt and pepper.
2. When the onions are soft — about 6 minutes — turn up the heat to medium and add the mushrooms. Season with another pinch of salt and pepper and cook until the mushrooms and onions are slightly browned and fragrant — about 3 minutes.
3. Remove from heat and add black beans and smash. You're looking for a rough mash.

Super Combo Burgers

4. Transfer the mixture to a mixing bowl and add the quinoa, beets, spices and stir.

5. Lastly, add the walnut meal a little at a time until the mixture is able enough to form into patties. Set in the fridge to chill while your oven preheats to 375 degrees F

6. Coat a baking sheet with olive oil. Form mixture into roughly 8-9 patties. I use a peanut butter jar lid lined with plastic wrap to get the perfect shape. You can also just take handfuls and mash them into loose patties.

7. Arrange burgers on a baking sheet and brush or spray the tops with olive oil. Bake at 375 for a total of 30-45 minutes, gently flipping at the halfway mark. Cook longer to dry them out even more and achieve more crisp.

8. Serve on small buns or atop mixed greens with desired toppings. See notes for freezing instructions.

Made in the USA
Las Vegas, NV
03 November 2022